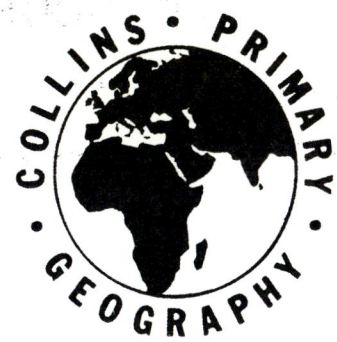

COLLINS · PRIMARY · GEOGRAPHY

World Watch 3

A World of Change

Planet Earth

Seas and Oceans

What is it like under the oceans?

Oceans cover about two-thirds of the Earth's surface, but we know less about them than any other part of the world. People are studying the oceans because they want to find out more about the animals that live in the water. They want to learn how the oceans affect the weather. They also want to know more about the ocean floor.

Exploring the oceans is difficult. There is plenty of light at the surface but below 200 metres it is almost completely dark.

The weight of the water is so heavy that people can only survive if they are in a submarine. It is also very cold.

Recently, scientists have discovered underwater vents. These pump fountains of boiling water and minerals into the ocean. Large numbers of animals live around these vents. Some of the animals have shells and look like crabs and shrimps. There are also huge worms that have no mouths or stomachs.

▼ *In most places, the ocean floor is about five kilometers below the surface of the water.*

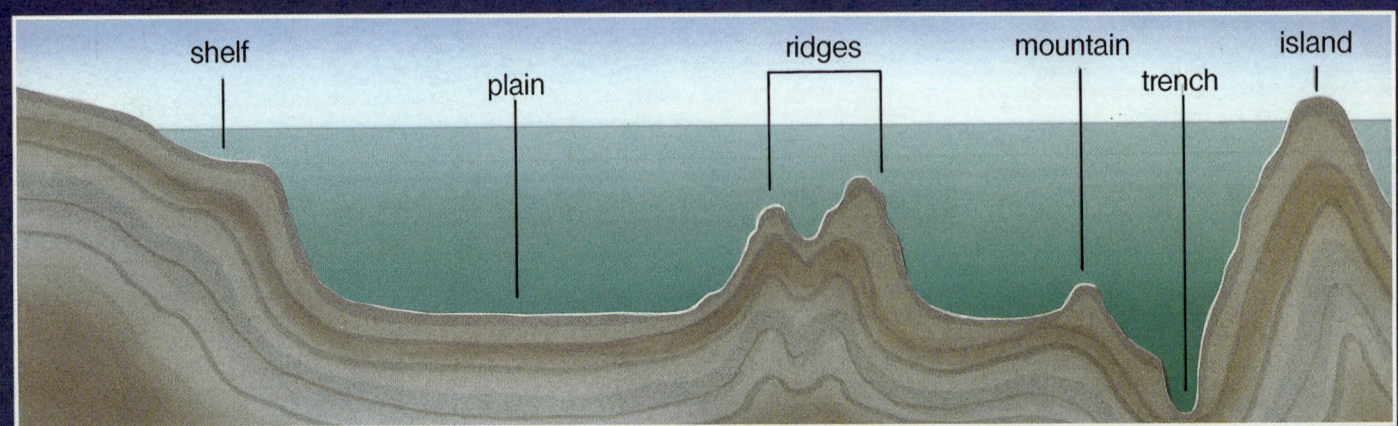

shelf   plain   ridges   mountain   trench   island

Talking and writing 💬✏️

Imagine you are the first person to use a new deep-sea submarine. Describe what you see as you go down to the ocean floor.

▲ Most plants and animals live within 100 metres of the ocean surface.

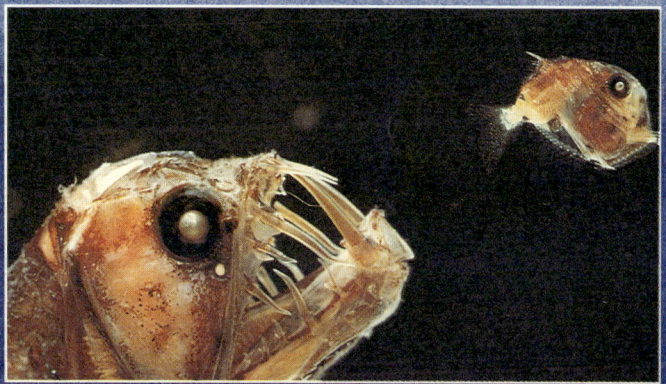

▲ Below 500 metres there are unusual fish which glow in the dark. This viperfish is hunting for food.

▲ Minerals from an underwater vent provide food for these deep-sea animals.

3

Why are the oceans important?

Weather

▲ *Storm clouds gather over the ocean.*

Near the Equator it is very hot. The sun heats up the surface of the ocean which makes the water evaporate quickly, causing violent storms. In other places, ocean currents are moved by the wind. One of these currents flows across the Atlantic to the west coast of Britain. Without it this country would be a lot colder in winter.

Using the evidence

1   Make a fact file for each of the oceans shown on the map.

2   Make a class scrapbook about the oceans using newspapers and magazines.

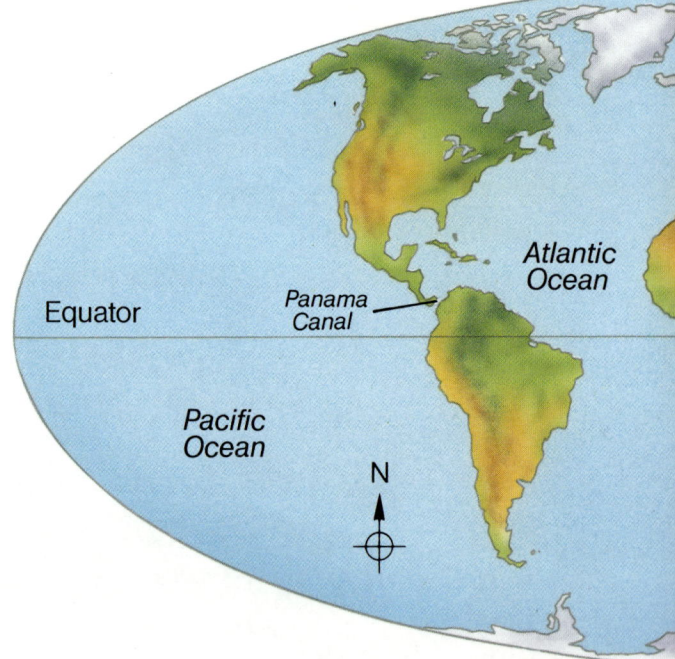

Atlantic Ocean

Equator

Panama Canal

Pacific Ocean

N

Fact file

◆ In winter the Arctic Ocean is completely covered by ice.

◆ The Marianas Trench in the Pacific Ocean is so deep (11,034 metres) that Mount Everest would fit inside it.

◆ There are more volcanoes under the ocean than there are on dry land.

Food
More fish are being caught now than ever before, and many species of fish are getting harder to find. This is because modern fishing boats drag long nets through the water. The nets catch everything in their paths and the fish have no chance to escape. In the Atlantic Ocean, stocks of herring and cod are very low. Around Antarctica so many whales have been killed that they are in danger of extinction.

▶ *Sorting through the catch.*

Transport

Most of the goods that are moved around the world are carried by ships. Tankers and bulk carriers are loaded with oil, coal, iron ore and other heavy cargoes. Some of the most important shipping routes cross the Atlantic and Indian Oceans.

◀ *A cargo ship.*

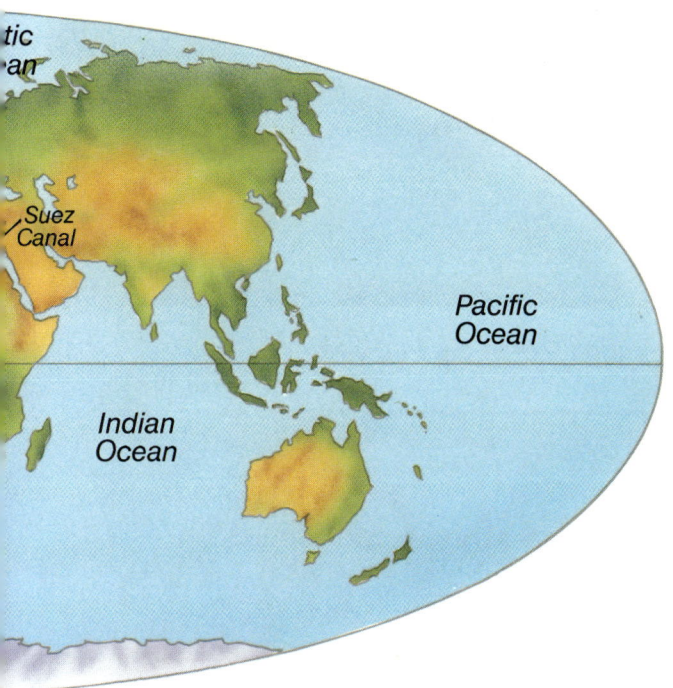

tic
an

Suez Canal

Pacific Ocean

Indian Ocean

Environment

▲ *A dolphin leaping through the waves.*

The oceans cover so much of the Earth's surface that they are the key to the health of our planet. Scientists are studying the birds, fish and other animals which live in the water. They are concerned that the oceans are becoming polluted with rubbish. One of the worst problems is in the Arctic Ocean where old nuclear submarines have been dumped.

5

What is a sea?

Around the edge of the oceans there are places where the water is shallower. These are known as seas.

Like oceans, seas are important habitats for fish and other animals. In some parts of the world, oil, gas and minerals have been found in rocks under the seabed. All these resources are very valuable to the countries around the seas.

▲ A coral reef in the Red Sea.

▲ Platforms are used to pump oil from under the seabed.

▶ There are seas around the edges of the oceans.

Mapwork

Using an atlas, name some of the countries around each of the seas in the table below.

Atlantic Ocean	Pacific Ocean	Indian Ocean
North Sea	Sea of Japan	Red Sea
Mediterranean Sea	South China Sea	The Gulf
Gulf of Mexico	Coral Sea	Arabian Sea
Caribbean Sea	Tasman Sea	Timor Sea

The North Sea

The North Sea is the busiest sea in the world. Thousands of ships cross it every day. There are also over 50 million people who live around the shores of the North Sea and the rivers which flow into it.

As a result the North Sea is very dirty. Fumes from the air, oil from ships and chemicals from sewage have polluted the water. Fish are diseased and birds are dying. Countries around the North Sea have now passed laws to try and make the water cleaner. A lot more still needs to be done.

▼ Most parts of the North Sea are very shallow.

- The North Sea contains three per cent of the world's fish stocks.
- In 1988, thousands of seals were killed by a mystery illness.
- Five thousand ships use the North Sea at any one time.
- There are 150 oil and gas platforms in the North Sea.

Things to do - - - - - - - - - - -

1 Make a list of the main rivers which flow into the North Sea.

2 How do people use the North Sea?

You have learnt

- ◆ about the features of the oceans and the sea bed
- ◆ why the oceans are important to us
- ◆ that seas and oceans are polluted.

Wearing Away the Land

Rivers

How do rivers shape the land?

▲ *This canoeist is being carried along by the force of the water. All he has to do is steer clear of the rocks!*

Rivers play a major part in shaping and moulding the land. As streams and rivers flow downhill, they wear away tiny pieces of rock on the river bed. They also eat into the earth banks on either side of the channel. The tiny particles of rock and earth bounce and scrape along the river bed wearing it away even more.

A lot of the material which is carried along by the water is dropped somewhere else. Some of it slowly builds up into banks of sand, mud and gravel in the middle of the river. In other places, the material is dropped in lakes and reservoirs. Over long periods of time, these fill up and turn into dry land.

▲ **Erosion:** *Rivers cut into the land creating valleys with steep sides.*

▲ **Transportation:** *Flood waters are so powerful they can carry rocks, boulders and whole trees downstream.*

▶ **Deposition:** *Rivers drop gravel and mud which build up in banks.*

Talking and writing

1 List the words which describe how rivers move and how they shape the land.
2 Make a river dictionary. Draw pictures to go with your words.

How can we control rivers?

The Mississippi River is over 3,000 kilometres long. It flows southwards across the United States of America draining water from half the country. The Mississippi is an important route for shipping.

In the past, the Mississippi was very shallow and used to flood the surrounding land after heavy rain. The river was also constantly changing its channel as it meandered towards the sea.

A hundred years ago, a team of river engineers tried to control the Mississippi. They wanted to make the channel deeper so that the river would be safe for shipping. They also wanted to protect nearby farms, towns and factories from floods. A lot of time and money has been spent on this work.

▲ The Mississippi was a dangerous river for shipping because it was very shallow and there were a lot of sandbanks.

Dykes	Levees	Cut-offs	Boxes
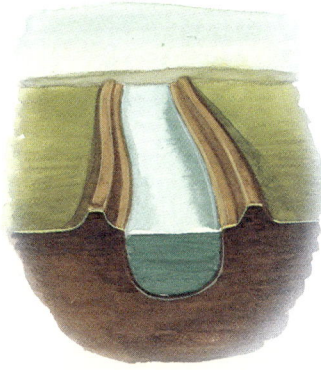	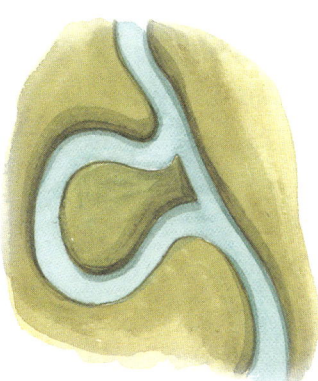		
Dykes along one side of the river force the water to cut a deeper channel on the opposite side.	Huge earth and clay banks called levees hold back the flood water.	New channels cut off some of the meanders so the water can flow faster.	The sides and bottom of the channel are lined with concrete boxes to make them stronger.

Dykes, levees and dams have been built. The channel has been straightened and lined with concrete. People believed that it was safe to live near the Mississippi. However, in 1993, after three months of heavy rain, the river rose higher and higher. It broke its banks, flooded houses and destroyed crops. Whole communities were wiped out. Now some people are questioning whether it will ever be possible to tame the Mississippi.

They think the river should be allowed to flood as it did in the past and believe the levees and boxes only trap the water and make things worse.

Using the evidence

Design the front page of a newspaper about the 1993 floods. Include reports from local residents who have lost their homes and from a river engineer who has flown over the area.

▼ Flooded farmland in 1993.

Finding out about rivers

Last year, the children from St Mark's Primary School went to Devon in south-west England. They stayed at a Field Study Centre so they could find out about the local environment. One of the places they visited was the River Dart. As part of their project the children tried to find out the answers to these questions.

1 In which compass direction does the river flow?
2 How wide is the river at three different places?
3 Is the river bed flat between the banks?
4 Are there any particles being carried along by the water?
5 Does the water flow at the same speed in the middle of the river as it does at the edges?
6 What plants grow on the river bank?
7 Is there any evidence of fish or animal life?
8 Are there any clues that the water level changes?

▼ *The children used this equipment when they studied the River Dart.*

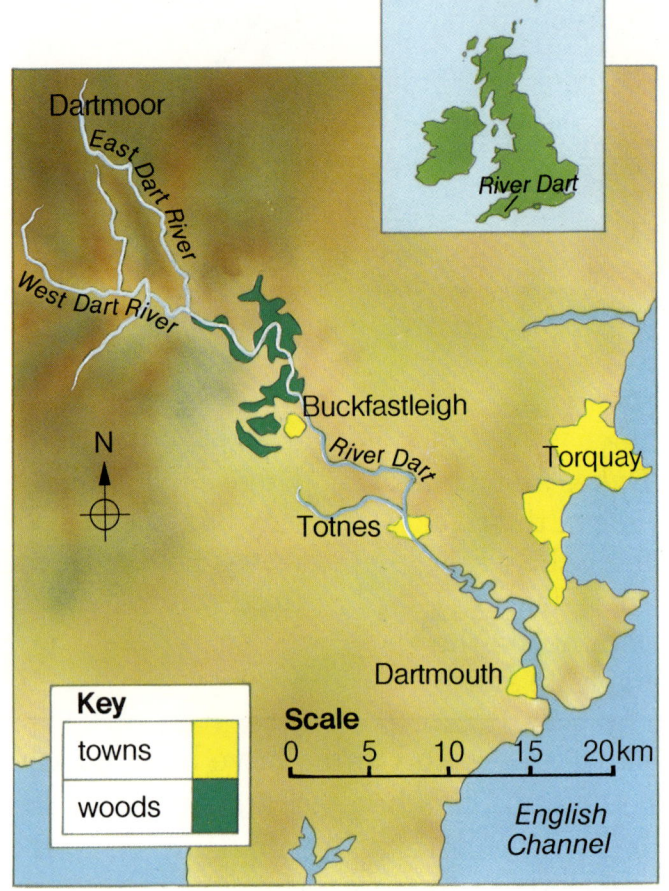

Dartmoor
East Dart River
West Dart River
River Dart
Buckfastleigh
Torquay
Totnes
N
Dartmouth
River Dart

Key
| towns | |
| woods | |

Scale
0   5   10   15   20km

English Channel

Things to do ✂ --------------

Decide which piece of equipment the children would need to answer the questions in the box on the left.

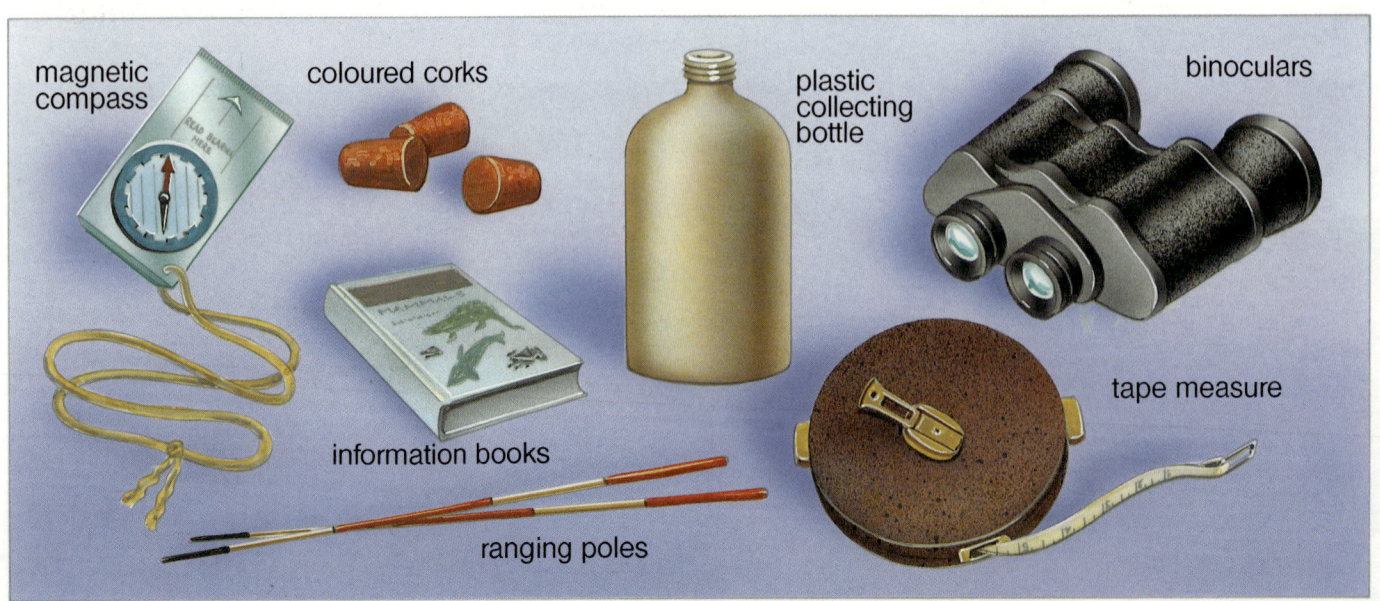

magnetic compass

coloured corks

plastic collecting bottle

binoculars

information books

ranging poles

tape measure

▲ *The children found that the river was seven metres at its widest part.*

▲ *One child used a plastic bottle to collect a sample of river water.*

Results of our River Study

We spent Tuesday at the river. We had to measure carefully and make observations using a compass. We found that the river flowed from north to south. In places it was three metres wide. The ranging pole showed the water was half a metre deep. It was flowing quite fast and it was cloudy with fine silt. We could see water weed and animal burrows along the bank.

When the children returned to the Study Centre, they recorded their results on a computer data file. They also looked at local maps to trace the route of the river from source to mouth. Then the children looked in books to find out more about the plants and animals which they had seen on the river bank. If there is a river near your school, you could make a similar study.

You have learnt

◆ that rivers are a major influence on the landscape
◆ how people try to control rivers
◆ how to study a river.

Weather

The Seasons

What are the seasons?

Although the weather changes from day to day, there is a pattern of seasons over the year. In winter, the weather is often cold and the days are dark and short. In summer, the weather is much warmer and the days are long and bright. Spring is the time when plants begin to grow and birds build their nests. Fruit and other crops are harvested in the autumn.

The changing seasons give a pattern to our lives. They affect the clothes we wear, the things we do and the places we visit. There are also seasonal festivals such as Christmas, Passover and Divali which mark out the year.

> ### Talking and writing
>
> 1 What clues show you what season it is?
>
> 2 Decide which season is shown in each of the photographs on page 15.
>
> 3 Make a chart showing which calendar months fit each season.

▼ *Changes in sunshine and temperature affect the life cycle of animals and plants.*

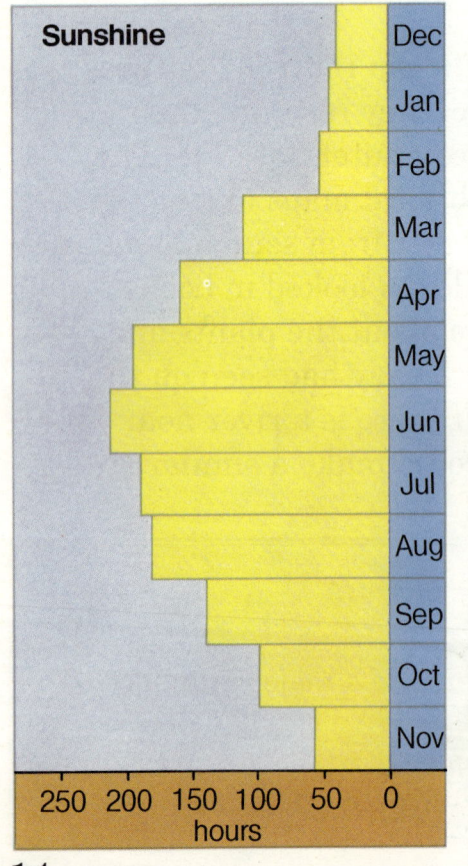

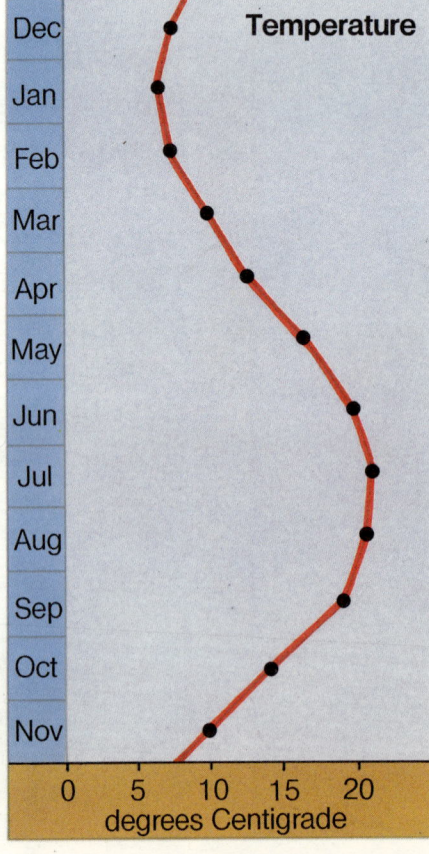

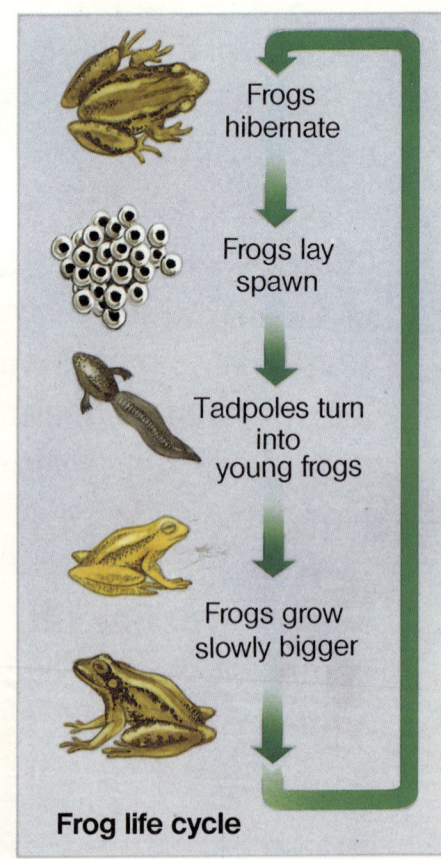

Frog life cycle

14

A

B

C

D

Do all places have the same seasons?

In the United Kingdom we have four seasons of equal length. Some other parts of the world have a different pattern of seasons. This affects how people live and the crops they can grow.

Using the evidence

Draw two heads and in speech bubbles write what you would like about the weather in the Mediterranean and South-East Asia.

Mediterranean climate in southern Europe

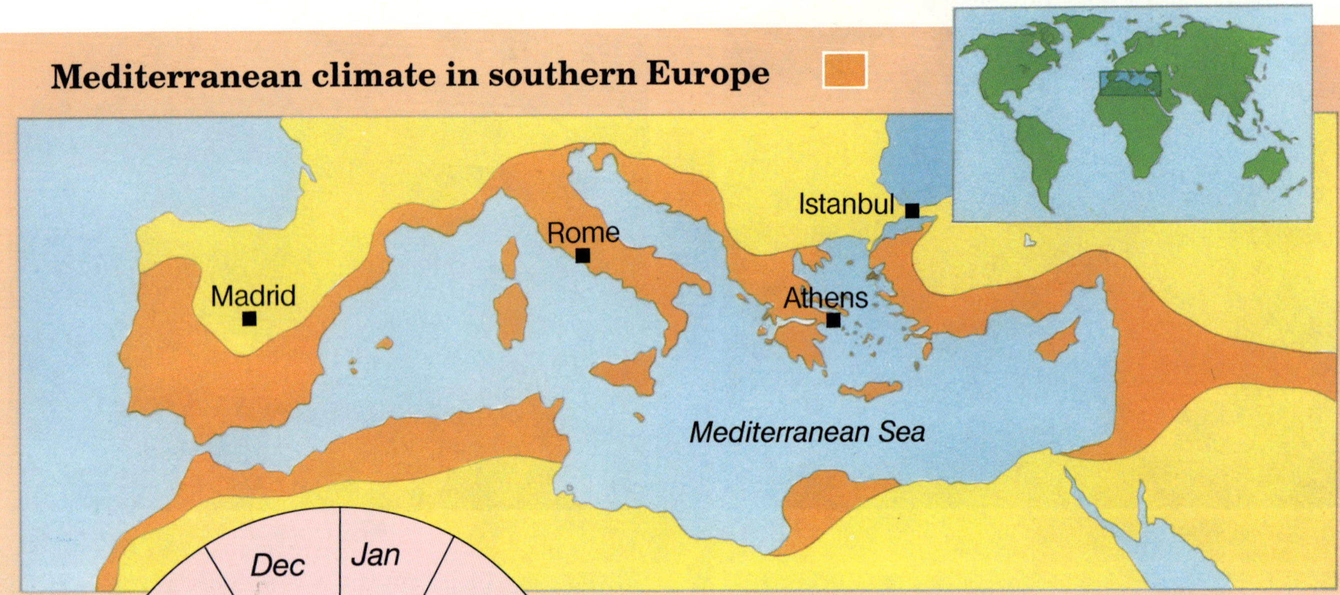

Istanbul

Rome

Madrid

Athens

Mediterranean Sea

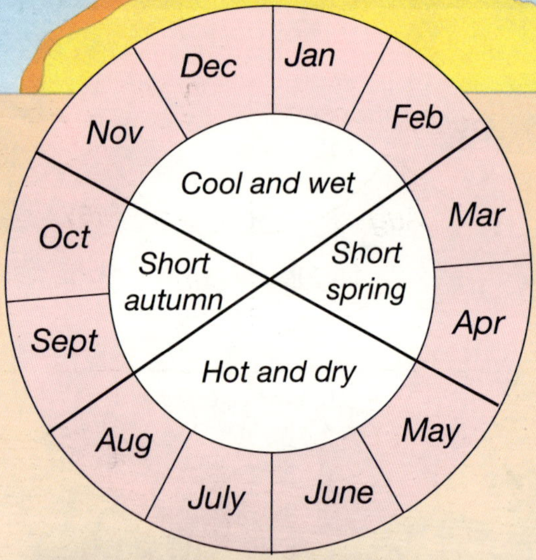

Dec / Jan / Feb / Mar / Apr / May / June / July / Aug / Sept / Oct / Nov

Cool and wet

Short autumn

Short spring

Hot and dry

Summer in the Mediterranean.

"Summer is a time of scorching heat. The countryside is alive with the humming of insects and the crackling of dry grass. In the fields the crops are ready to harvest.

During the day the whole land is flooded with light. The glare of the sun is thrown back from the white rocks. The streams dry up and only tough plants can survive in the heat.

We used to sleep in the afternoon because it was so hot and sit out on the terrace in the evening because it was still comfortably warm. The skies were clear and starry."

(Adapted from *Mehmet My Hawk* by Yashar Kemal, HarperCollins Publishers)

◀ *A Mediterranean landscape in Italy.*

Monsoon climate in South-East Asia

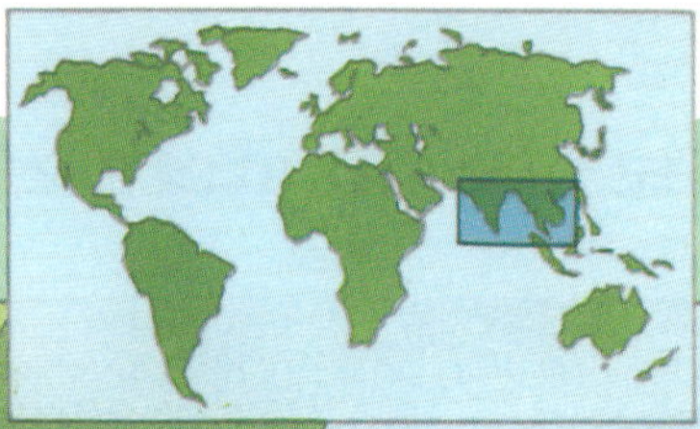

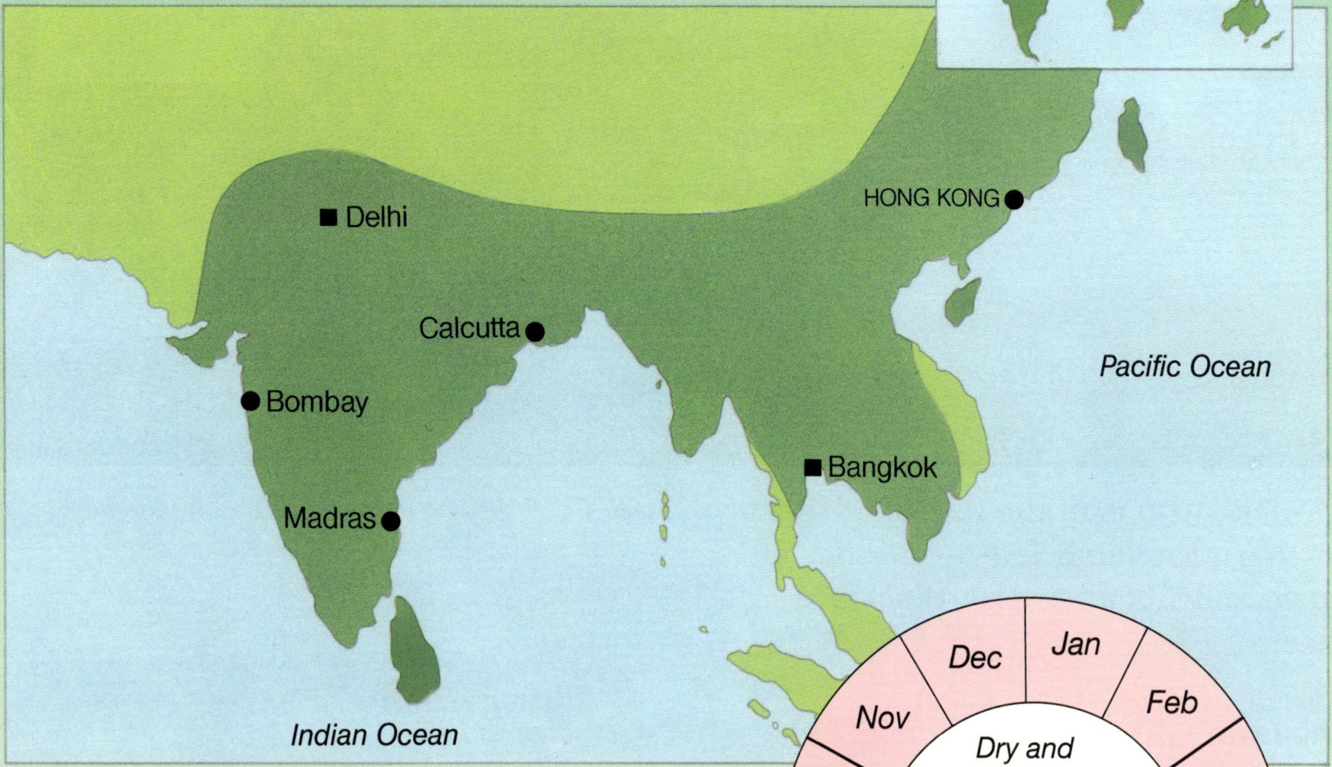

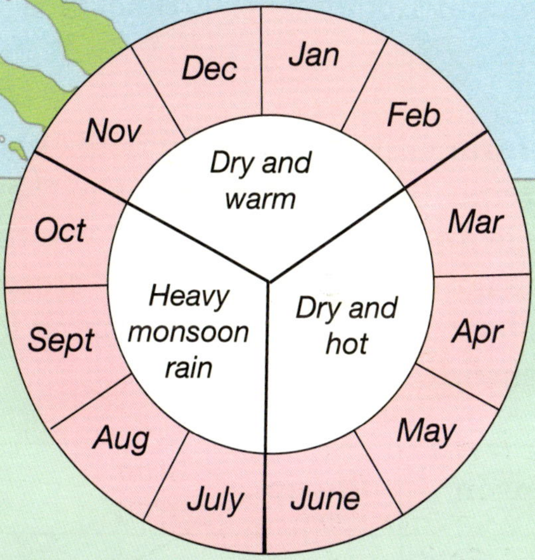

HONG KONG

Delhi

Calcutta

Bombay

Bangkok

Madras

Pacific Ocean

Indian Ocean

The monsoon rains arrive.

Dry and warm — Nov, Dec, Jan, Feb
Dry and hot — Mar, Apr, May, June
Heavy monsoon rain — July, Aug, Sept, Oct

"A hot wind blew through our bungalow day and night from the huge open plain. Then the clouds began to bank up and bank up and there was an unbearable feeling of pressure.

The rains came down with a terrific force such as you hardly ever see in Europe. This would probably go on for two or three days and the whole area round the house turned green.

We used to plant seeds and in no time at all they were up and flowering. An extraordinary life burst out, with frogs and toads hopping about the paths. At first it was absolutely wonderful."

(Adapted from *Plain Tales of the Raj* by Charles Allen, Futura Publications)

▲ Monsoon rains are vital for crops such as rice. One thousand million people depend on rice grown during the monsoon for their food.

How are farmers affected by the seasons?

Hawick Farm is in the Pennine Hills in northern England. The farmer has 50 cattle and 1,000 Scottish Blackface sheep.

The farm is surrounded by fields in a sheltered valley. Above the farm there is a large area of open moorland where the soil is not good enough to grow crops. This land is used as rough grazing for the sheep.

▲ *Cows grazing in the fields around the farm.*

Things to do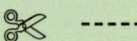

Draw three season dials to show the jobs the farmer has to do to look after a) the sheep, b) the cattle, and c) the farm.

Season	Sheep	Cattle	Other jobs
Spring	Sheep brought down from the moors for lambing. Lambs marked and tails removed.	Calves born. Some cattle sold at market.	Muck spread in the fields to help the grass grow.
Summer	Sheep dipped to stop disease. Wool clipped and sold. Sheep taken back to the moors.	Mating of cows.	Haymaking.
Autumn	Sheep dipped again. Mating time.	Cattle put in the fields after haymaking.	Drains repaired in the fields.
Winter	Sheep fed by farmer during snowy weather.	Cattle fed on hay and turnips in the barns.	Repairs to stone walls.

How are seaside resorts affected by the seasons?

Whitby is a town on the coast of Yorkshire. It has a busy fishing harbour and a long sandy beach. Many people go to Whitby for their holidays. Some people visit the old abbey.

▼ *The number of visitors to Whitby Abbey.*

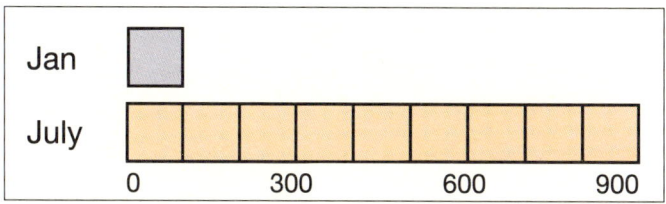

▲ *The ruins of Whitby Abbey. It was destroyed by Henry VIII in 1539.*

Summer	Winter
In summer Whitby is crowded with visitors who come from all parts of the UK and abroad.	In winter Whitby is much quieter, particularly when the wind brings rain and snow from the North Sea.

- Beach busy with tourists.
- Boat trips.
- Steam railway.
- Museum open every day.

- Beach empty.
- Sea too rough for boat trips.
- Railway line repaired.
- Museum only open at weekends.

Things to do - - - - - - - - - - -

Look at the pictures on this page. How does Whitby change from summer to winter?

You have learnt

- ◆ how the seasons are different
- ◆ about seasons around the world
- ◆ how people are affected by the seasons.

Settlement

Cities

What are cities like?

▲ *Skyscrapers in New York City.*

Cities are the largest of all settlements. They are busy, crowded places with hundreds of thousands of inhabitants.

During the day, people come to the city centre to buy things in the shops and work in the tall office blocks. As night falls, people leave work and go to restaurants, theatres and cinemas to enjoy themselves. The streets are full of bright lights from the shops and advertisements. Away from the centre, it is quieter. The suburbs spread out into the countryside. There is more space there for houses and gardens, shops and parks.

▼ *There are advantages and disadvantages to city life.*

Cities are connected to other places by motorways and express trains. Most cities also have airports. The different parts of a city are linked together by roads, railways, trams or underground trains. So many people want to move around that the roads are often jammed with traffic. Other problems include noise, fumes and vandalism.

Talking and writing

1 In what ways are cities different from towns and villages?

2 Draw a picture of yourself. Write what you think about city life in a speech bubble.

There are lots of jobs in the city centre.

All the fumes from the traffic are bad for my health.

We like living in the city because there are lots of things to do in the evening.

It's very noisy and crowded where we live.

I have come to the city to study at university.

There are no open spaces to play ball games where I live.

How are cities changing?

Around the world, many cities are getting bigger and bigger as more and more people arrive from the country. Some people are attracted to cities because they think they will find a better life there. Others are forced to move out of their villages by war, drought and famine.

Using the evidence

Look at the table on the right. Draw a bar chart to show the changes in the number of people living in each city.

City	Millions of people	
	1980	2000 (estimate)
New York, USA	16	17
Mexico City, Mexico	14	16
São Paulo, Brazil	12	22
Buenos Aires, Argentina	10	13
London, UK	8	7
Cairo, Egypt	7	11
Bombay, India	8	18
Shanghai, China	12	17
Tokyo, Japan	22	28

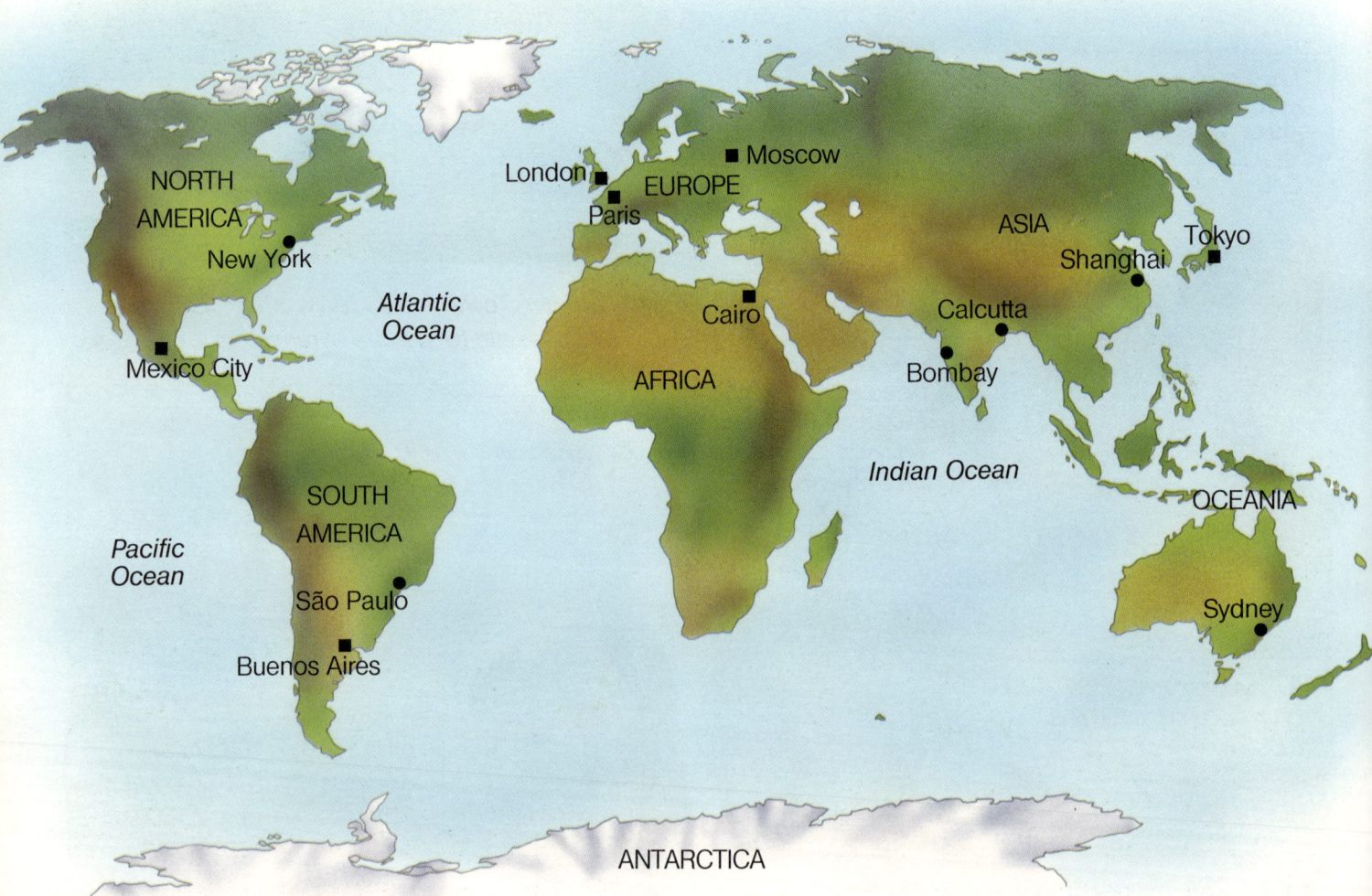

▲ Cities around the world.

The story of Cairo

The city of Cairo developed on the Nile delta because desert routes crossed the river there. Today, Cairo is the capital city of Egypt and is the largest city in Africa. It has modern office blocks, flats and hotels. There are also many ancient buildings. These include an old fort, mosques and markets.

Cairo is growing rapidly. Every week about 5,000 people arrive from the countryside looking for work and somewhere to live. They crowd into small flats and camp in empty spaces on the flat roof tops. New houses, hospitals, roads and schools are being built all the time but it is difficult to provide enough for everyone.

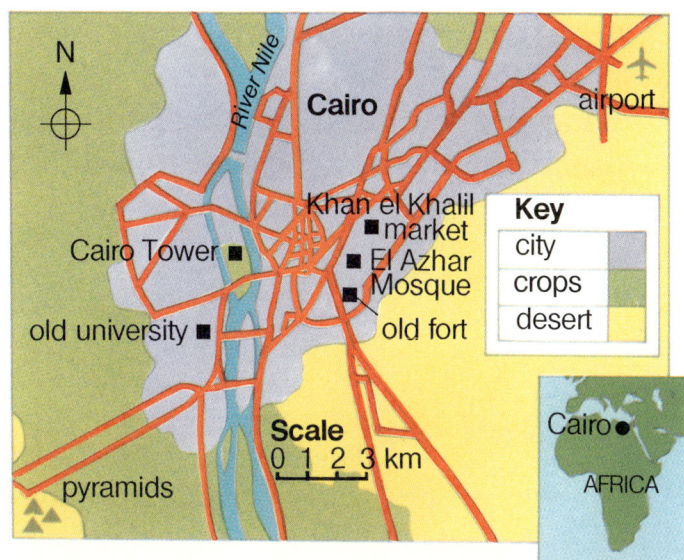

▲ The Cairo Tower is 180 metres high. On a clear day it is possible to see the pyramids from the top.

▲ The Khan el Khalil market is in the centre of Cairo.

▲ The El Azhar mosque was built nearly one thousand years ago.

The story of London

London was built at a crossing point on the River Thames. Low hills on the north bank of the Thames provided a dry site above the marshes. Ships could sail up the river carrying goods from other parts of Europe.

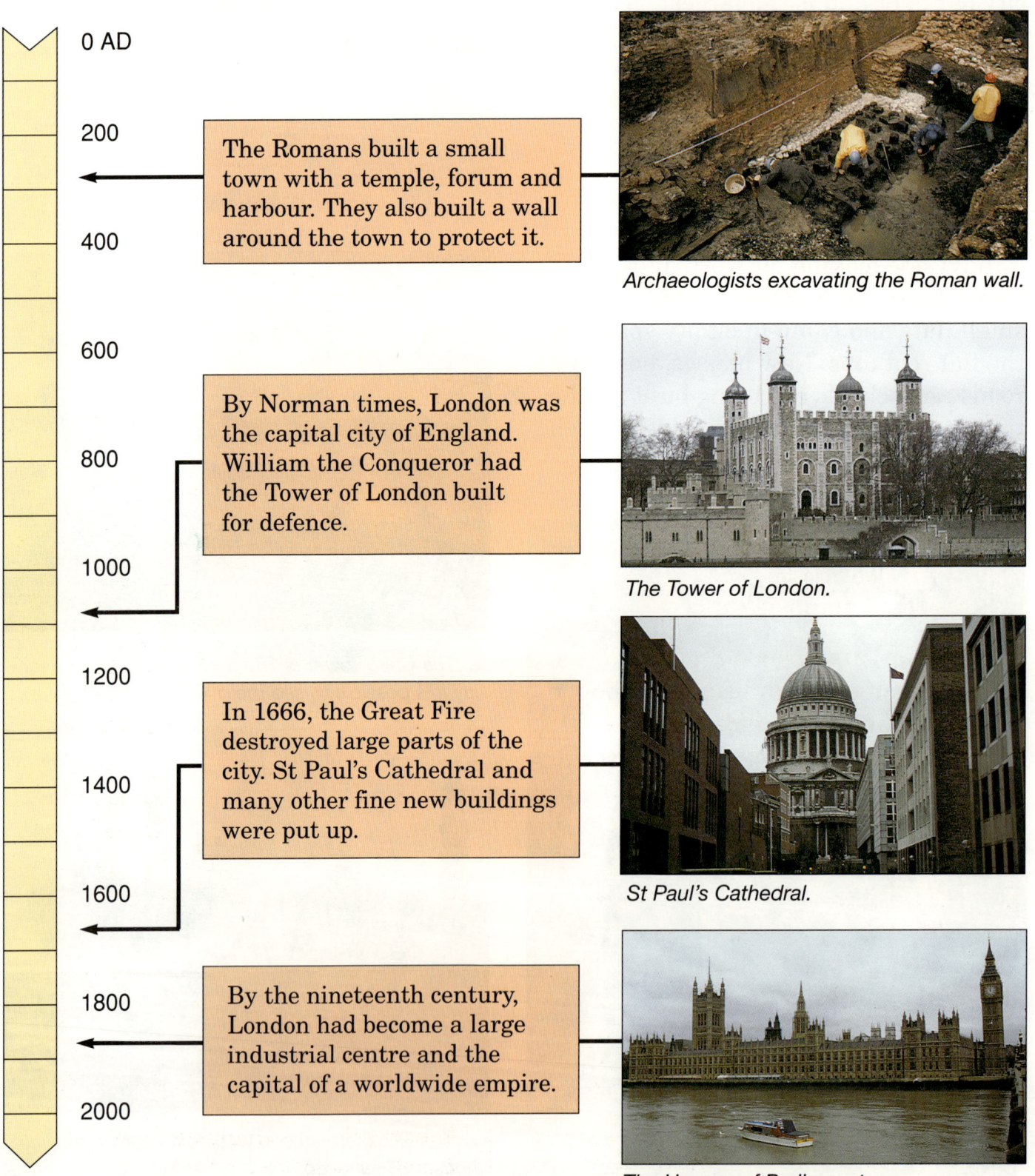

0 AD

200

400

The Romans built a small town with a temple, forum and harbour. They also built a wall around the town to protect it.

Archaeologists excavating the Roman wall.

600

800

1000

By Norman times, London was the capital city of England. William the Conqueror had the Tower of London built for defence.

The Tower of London.

1200

1400

1600

In 1666, the Great Fire destroyed large parts of the city. St Paul's Cathedral and many other fine new buildings were put up.

St Paul's Cathedral.

1800

2000

By the nineteenth century, London had become a large industrial centre and the capital of a worldwide empire.

The Houses of Parliament.

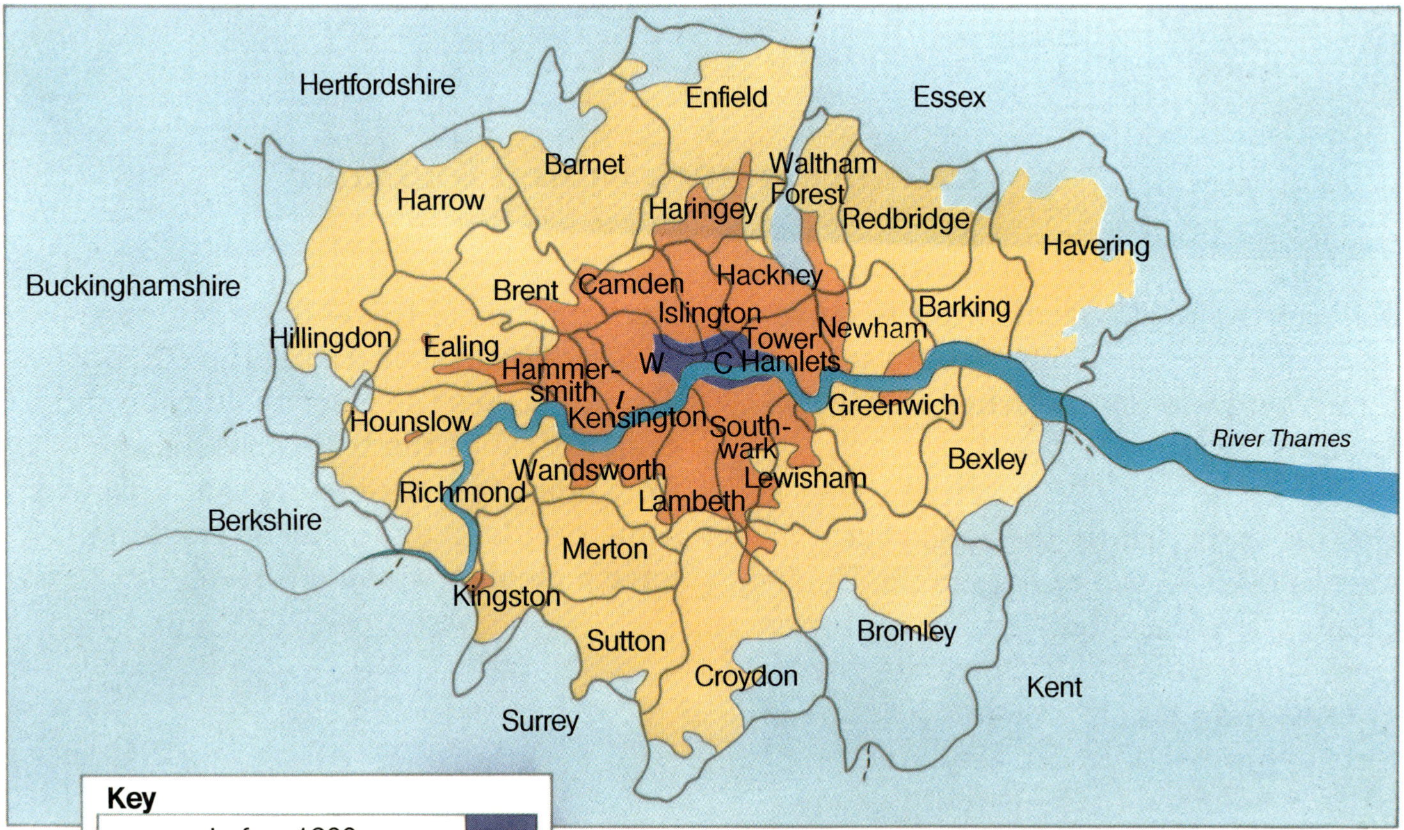

The map shows the boroughs of London, colour-coded by the period of their development.

London boroughs

Hertfordshire

Enfield

Essex

Harrow · Barnet

Waltham Forest

Haringey

Redbridge

Havering

Buckinghamshire

Brent · Camden · Hackney

Islington

Barking

Hillingdon · Ealing

Hammersmith · W · C · Tower Hamlets · Newham

Kensington

Greenwich

Hounslow

Southwark

Bexley

Wandsworth

Richmond · Lambeth · Lewisham

Berkshire

Merton

Kingston

Bromley

Sutton

Croydon

Kent

Surrey

River Thames

Key		
	before 1800	
	19th century	
	20th century	
The City	C	
Westminster	W	

The population of London reached a peak of about eight and a half million people in the 1950s. Since then, the numbers have fallen as people moved out to new towns with more modern houses and plenty of space.

▶ *The main cities of the UK.*

North Sea

N

Glasgow ● ■ Edinburgh

Newcastle ●

Belfast ■

Leeds ●

Manchester ●

Birmingham ●

Cardiff ■ · London ■

Bristol ●

English Channel

Things to do ✂ - - - - - - - - - - - - - -

1 Find out one thing about each of the cities marked on the UK map.

2 Using maps, words and pictures, tell the story of your nearest city.

You have learnt

◆ how cities are different from other places
◆ how cities are changing
◆ how to describe a city.

Transport

Transport Links

How are places linked together?

All over the world people want to move around. They travel for work, to see family and friends and when they go on holiday.

Getting from Britain to France has always been difficult because the English Channel creates a barrier. For centuries ferries provided a link. Since the 1920s, aircraft have also been used. Now a railway tunnel has been built and Britain is linked to the rest of Europe.

Each method of travel has advantages and disadvantages. Using the Channel Tunnel makes the journey quicker and easier because the train goes directly from one city centre to another. However, some people like to relax on the ferry, have a meal or watch a film.

Dover

English Channel

ENGLAND

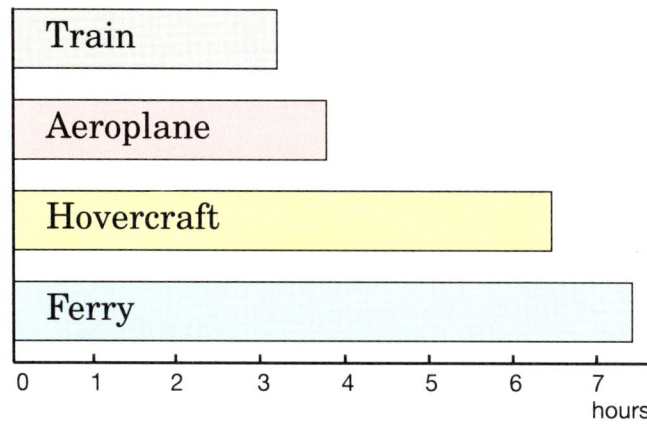

▲ Travel times from London to Paris.

▶ In 1994, trains from London could travel direct to Paris and Brussels for the first time.

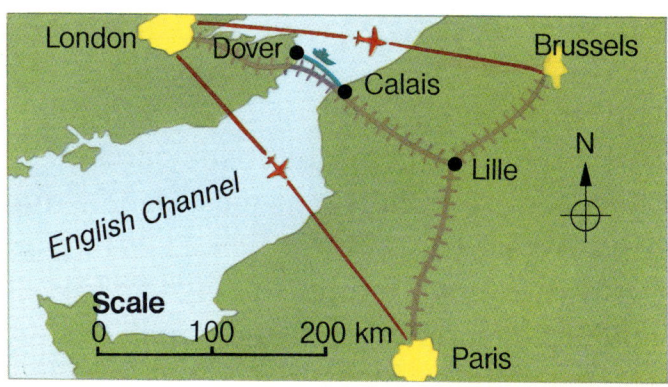

Talking and writing

What are the advantages of crossing the Channel by train, plane, hovercraft and ferry?

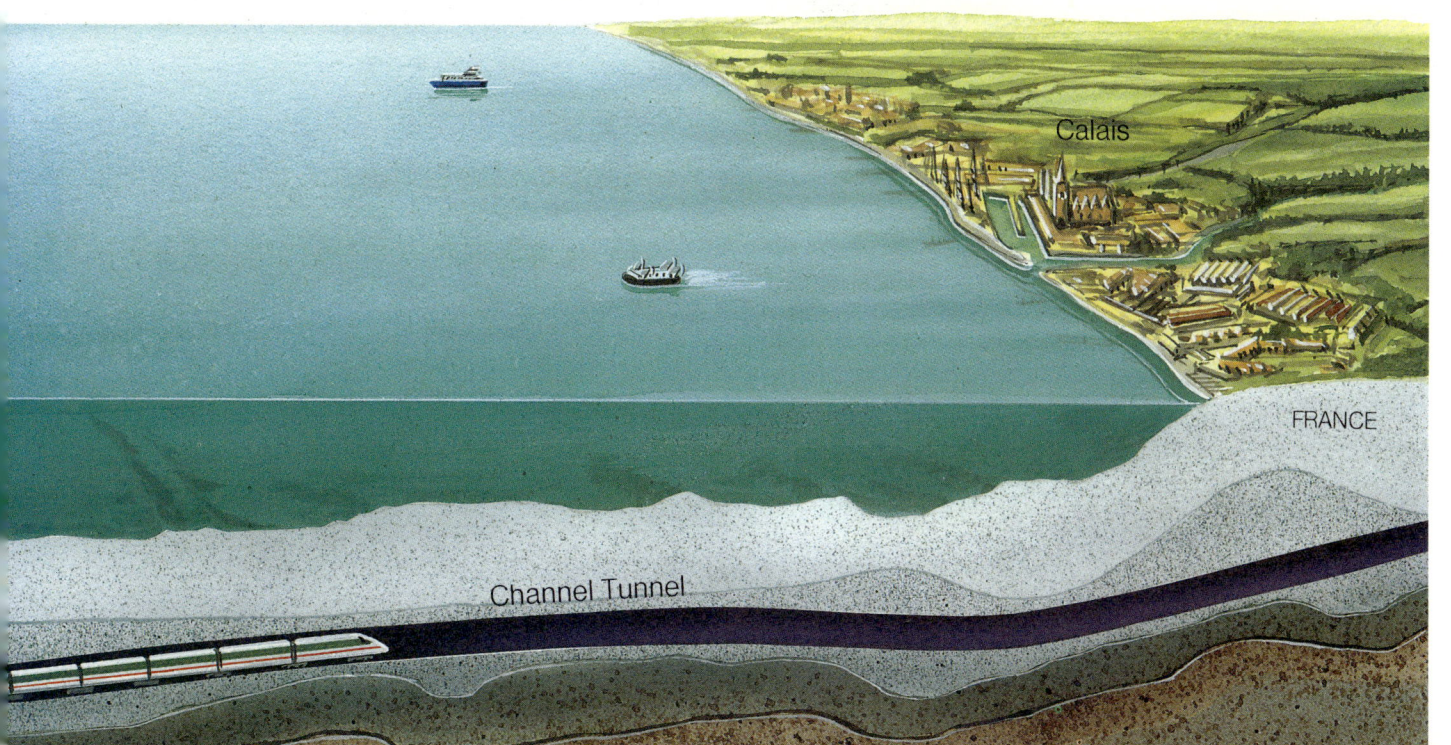

How are transport links changing?

Railways

Until 150 years ago, the roads across Europe were so bad that most people did not travel far from their homes. When the railways were built during the last century, it suddenly became much easier to move about. Heavy goods, like coal, could also be moved around in large quantities.

Now the railways of Europe are being improved with a new high-speed network. By the year 2010 most of the main cities in Europe will be linked together.

Using the evidence

How do you think the new high-speed rail network will change people's lives?

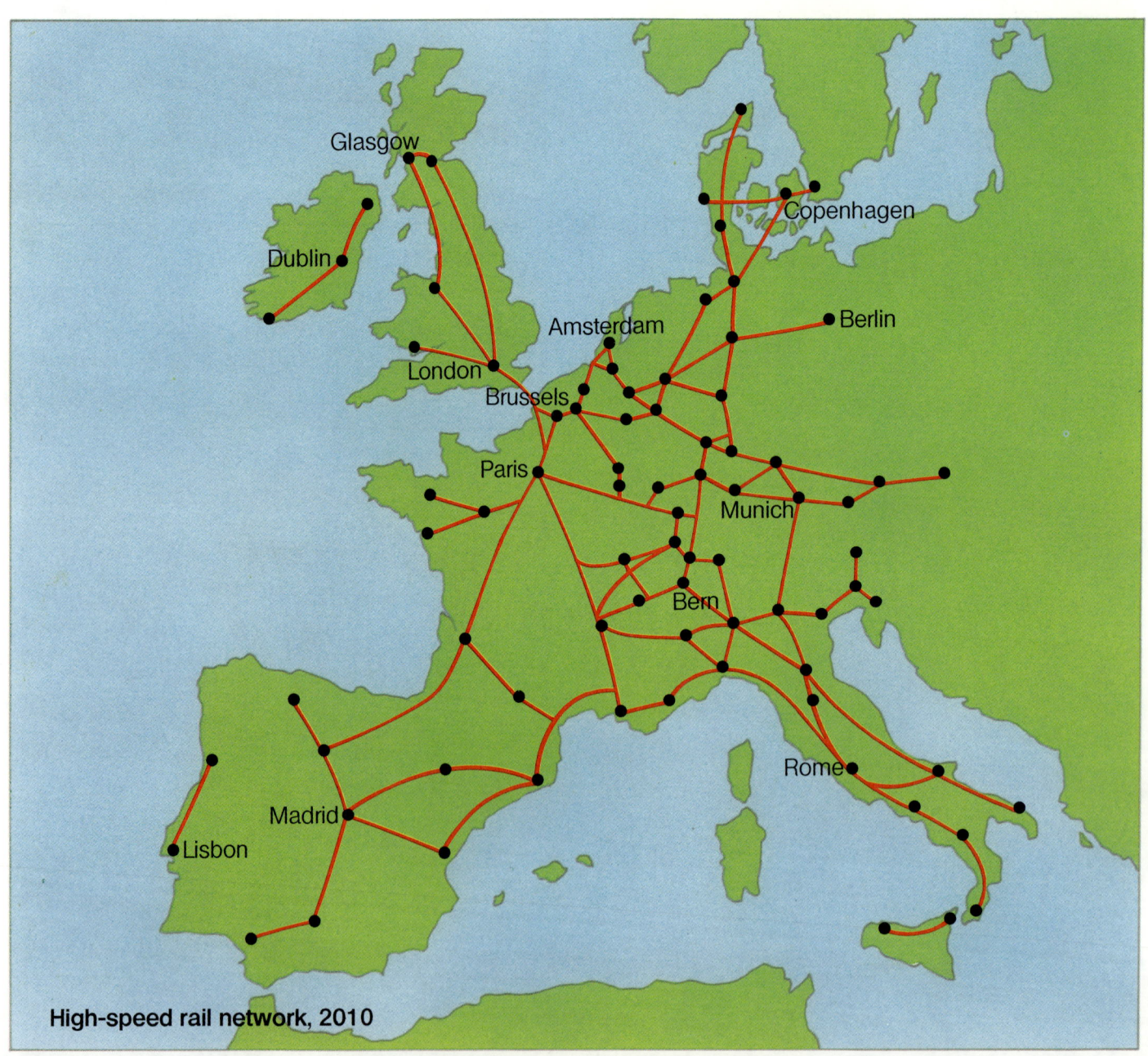

High-speed rail network, 2010

28

Air travel

One hundred years ago, people were still learning how to make aeroplanes. Now 500 million people a year travel around the world by air. Each year the numbers keep on growing.

When aircraft fly from place to place, they follow the same routes. The skies over Western Europe and North America are the busiest in the world. Huge planes, like the jumbo jet, fly on these routes. Each plane can carry over 500 people. In the future, bigger planes and more air terminals will be needed to cope with the demand.

Mapwork

N

Which places shown on the map are on three or more air routes?

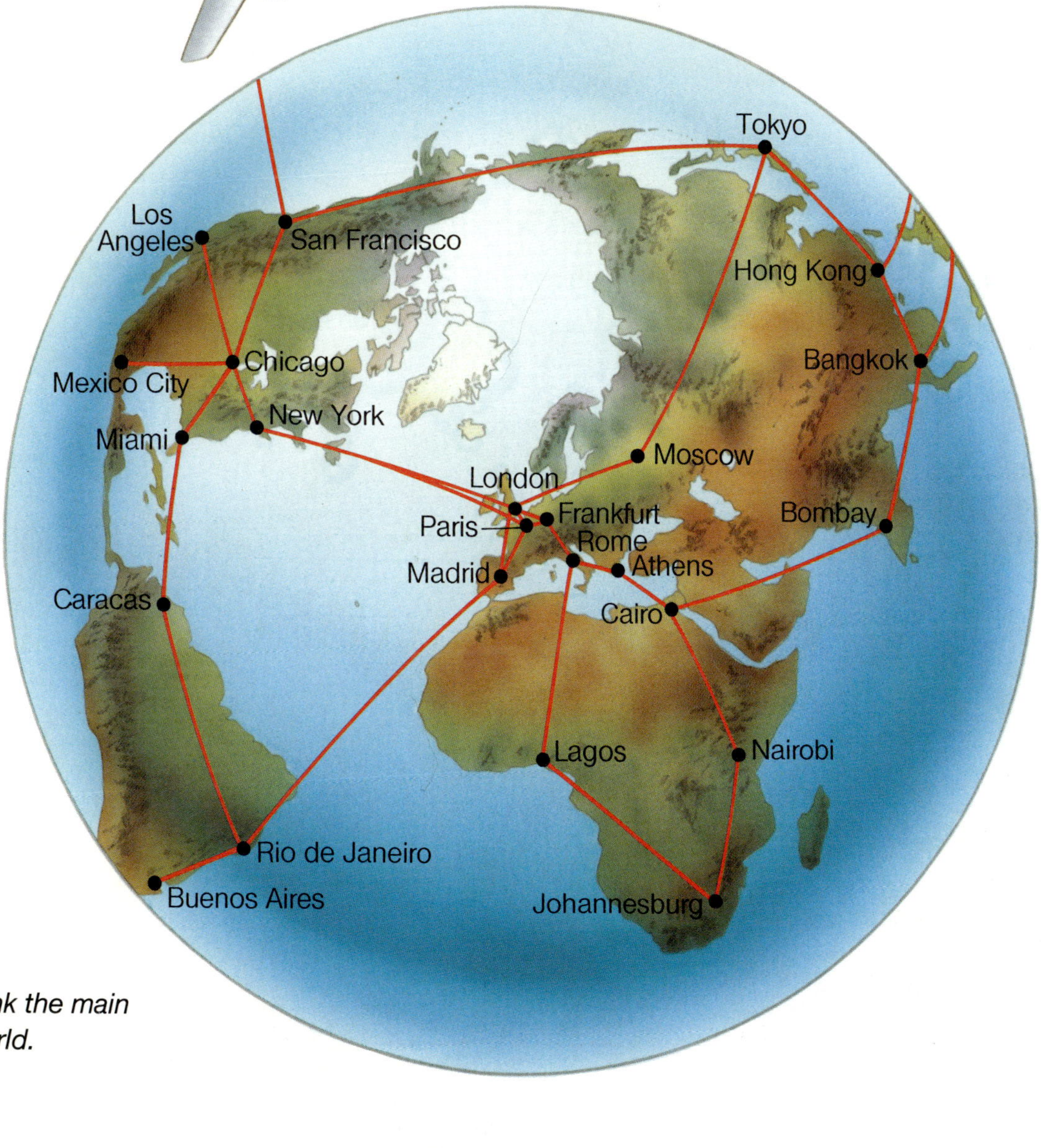

▲ Air routes link the main cities of the world.

Why do we use different methods of transport?

Janet Parker is travelling from Banchory in Scotland to stay with her aunt at Ryde on the Isle of Wight. Look at her journey on the map.

Types of transport

local bus

Intercity express train

aeroplane

underground

express coach

ferry

Things to do ✂ - - - - - - - - - - - -

1 Discuss why Janet uses a different type of transport for each part of her journey.

2 Use the scale on the map to work out how far Janet has to travel. Which are the quickest and slowest parts of Janet's journey? Why?

Banchory ● ● Aberdeen

SCOTLAND

● Edinburgh

ENGLAND

WALES

London ■

Portsmouth ●

Ryde ●
Isle of Wight

Scale
0   100   200   300   400   500   600 km

Times

Place	Time
Banchory	6.30 am
Aberdeen	8.00 am
Edinburgh	9.30 am
London, Heathrow	12.00 am
London, Victoria Coach Station	2.00 pm
Portsmouth	6.00 pm
Ryde	8.30 pm

30

Finding out about local transport

Children at a school in Truro, Cornwall found out about bus services in their area. Working from a map, they counted up the number of routes leading away from each town. Then they wrote a report saying which towns were easiest to reach.

> St. Austell, Truro and Bodmin have the best bus services in our area. There are routes leading in lots of different directions. Padstow, Gorran Haven and Falmouth only have one route and are hardest to reach.

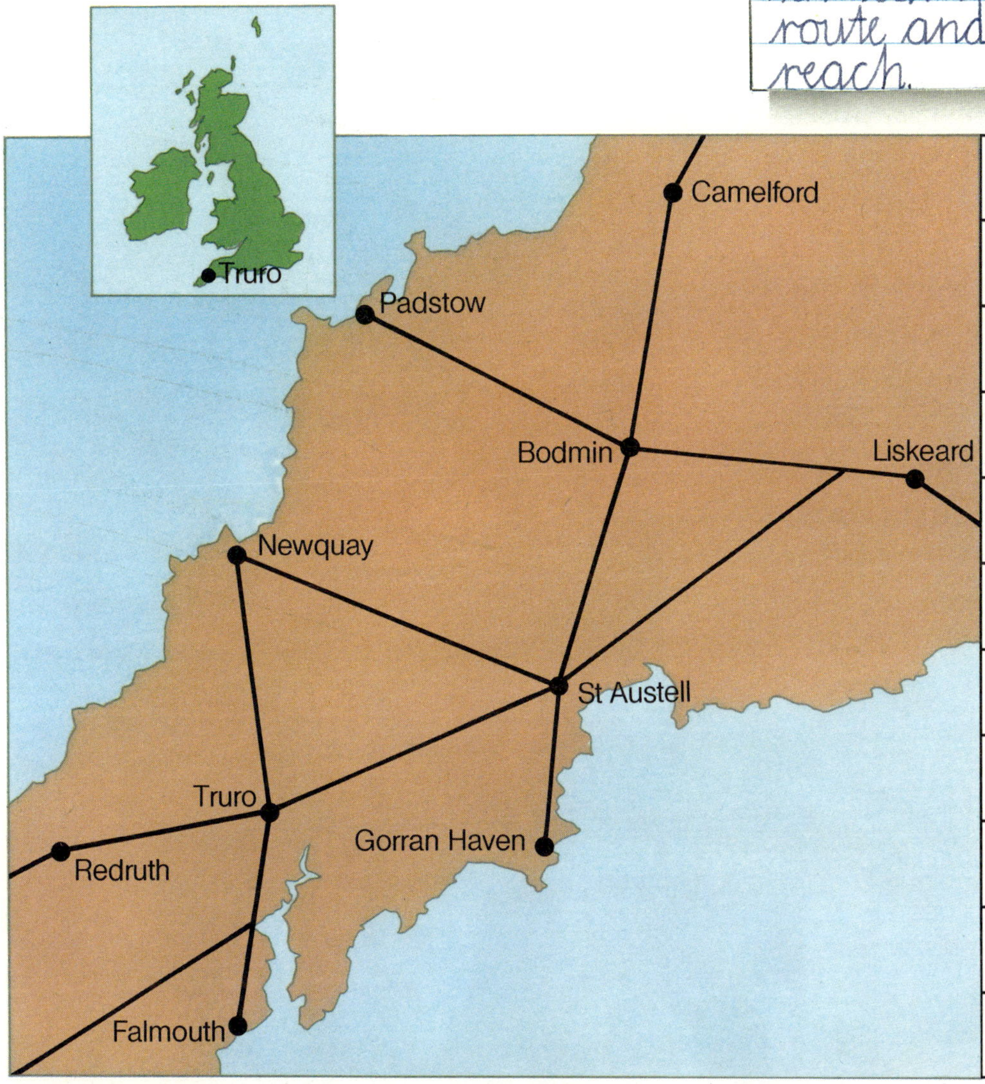

Place	Routes
Redruth	2
Newquay	2
Padstow	1
Camelford	2
Bodmin	4
Liskeard	2
St Austell	5
Gorran Haven	1
Truro	4
Falmouth	1

(Map of Cornwall showing bus routes between: Camelford, Padstow, Bodmin, Liskeard, Newquay, St Austell, Truro, Gorran Haven, Redruth, Falmouth. Inset map shows location of Truro in the UK.)

Things to do - - - - - - - - - - - - -

Draw a map showing where buses go in your area. Why do the routes stop and start where they do?

You have learnt

- ◆ why transport links are needed
- ◆ how transport links are changing
- ◆ how to study transport links in your area.

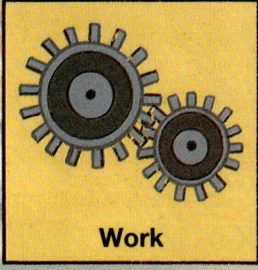

Work

Shops

Why do people buy and sell things?

Most people in the world cannot make and grow everything they need. They have to go to shops and markets to buy food, clothes and tools.

In some places, people put up stalls in markets where they sell the crops they have grown. However, most traders buy goods, like fruit or clothes, from farms and factories. They make their living by selling the goods at a higher price so they can make a profit.

Market stalls and small shops are often run as a family business. Supermarkets and chain stores usually belong to large companies. They provide jobs for a lot of people.

Talking and writing

1 In what way do the photographs all show similar activities?

2 What words describe what is happening in the photographs? Write a caption to go with each one.

33

How do goods reach the supermarkets?

Jane Ford works for a fruit importers in Lincolnshire. Her company buys fruit from abroad and sells it to supermarkets. The fruit the company imports changes with the seasons. However, some fruit like grapes, apples, oranges, melons, peaches and nectarines are usually available all year.

Jane starts work at 7.30 am. She begins by phoning supermarkets to find out how well fruit has been selling. Then she takes their orders. Sometimes she visits a fruit market or meets a new customer.

The importers is a busy place. Each day two or three large lorries arrive from Sheerness docks at the mouth of the River Thames. The fruit is unloaded as soon as it arrives.

▲ Checking oranges at the fruit importers. Any bad ones have to be taken out.

▲ Fruit in the cold store ready to go to the supermarkets.

Importing bananas

These are the stages involved in importing bananas from Jamaica. Most of the bananas sold in the UK come from the West Indies.

Growing

The bananas are grown on a plantation.

Packing

They are put into boxes at a pack house.

Jane has been doing her job for many years. "When I started most of our fruit went to small shops," she explains. "Now it goes to the supermarkets. They get all the best produce."

"The biggest change is that people can now buy fresh fruit all the year round. For example, in the past you only used to get grapes when they were in season. Now you can buy them all the time. When the harvest stops in one country it starts in another."

"The demand for grapes is highest just before Christmas and in the summer months when the weather is good. Sometimes fruit is sold at a very low price to encourage people to buy more. This is called a promotion. We sell the fruit for the best price we can get. It is much cheaper to buy and sell in large quantities."

▲ *Jane's company buys grapes from different countries at different times of the year.*

Using the evidence

1 Make a list of all the jobs people do to bring bananas to a British supermarket.

2 On your own map of the world, label and colour the countries where the importers buy grapes.

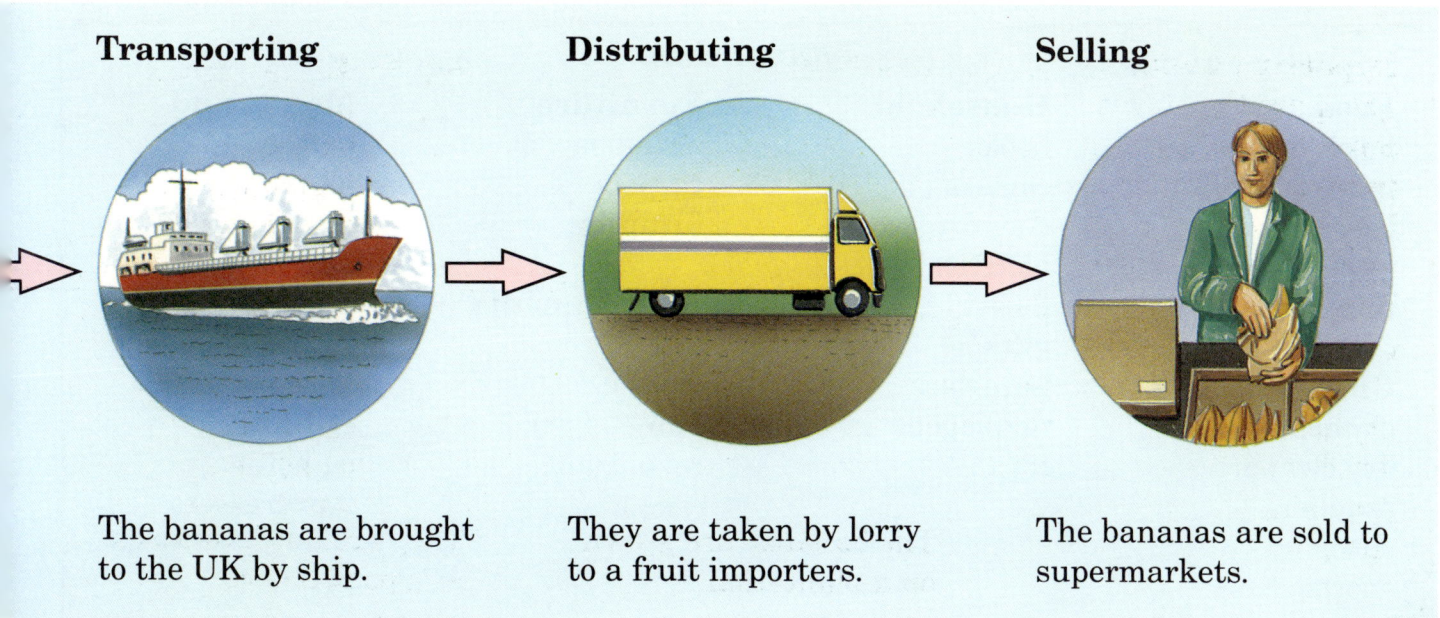

Transporting

The bananas are brought to the UK by ship.

Distributing

They are taken by lorry to a fruit importers.

Selling

The bananas are sold to supermarkets.

A local investigation

At Benwell in Newcastle the children made a study of the shops in their local High Street. First, they used a map to identify the different buildings. Then they visited the High Street and wrote down what each one was called. Afterwards they sorted the shops into different types using a list their teacher gave them. Some of the shops sold a lot of different things, so the children had to decide what was the most important.

Number	Name of shop
	Hindu Temple
170	Medical Centre
168	V. G. Mini Market
164	Newcastle Building Soc.
160	United Newsagent
156	Estate Agent
152	Scoop and Save Foods
148	Thompson Chemist
144	Arctic Frozen Foods
140	Boots Chemist
136	Newcastle Estate Agents
132	Carricks Bakers
128	Pineapple Fruit + Veg.
124	Cellar 5 Mini Market
118	Westo Stores Mini Market
112	Northern Rock Building Soc.
108	Gregg's Bakers
106	EMPTY
100	Marie Curie Cancer Care
96	Hill House Insurance
92	Barclay's Bank
72	Bingo Hall

Type of shop

Food
baker
butcher
greengrocer
health food
mini market

Clothes
clothes
dry cleaners
jewellers
shoes
sports

Household
books
cameras
chemist
electrical
florist
gifts
hardware
newsagent
toys

Furniture
antiques
carpets
furniture

Refreshments
café
fast food
pub
restaurant

Money and offices
bank
building society
estate agent
post office
travel agent

Others
eg hotel
hairdressers

When they returned to school, the children coloured their maps. They used a different colour for each type of shop and added a key. They also added up the totals to find which type of shop was most common and made a bar chart of the results.

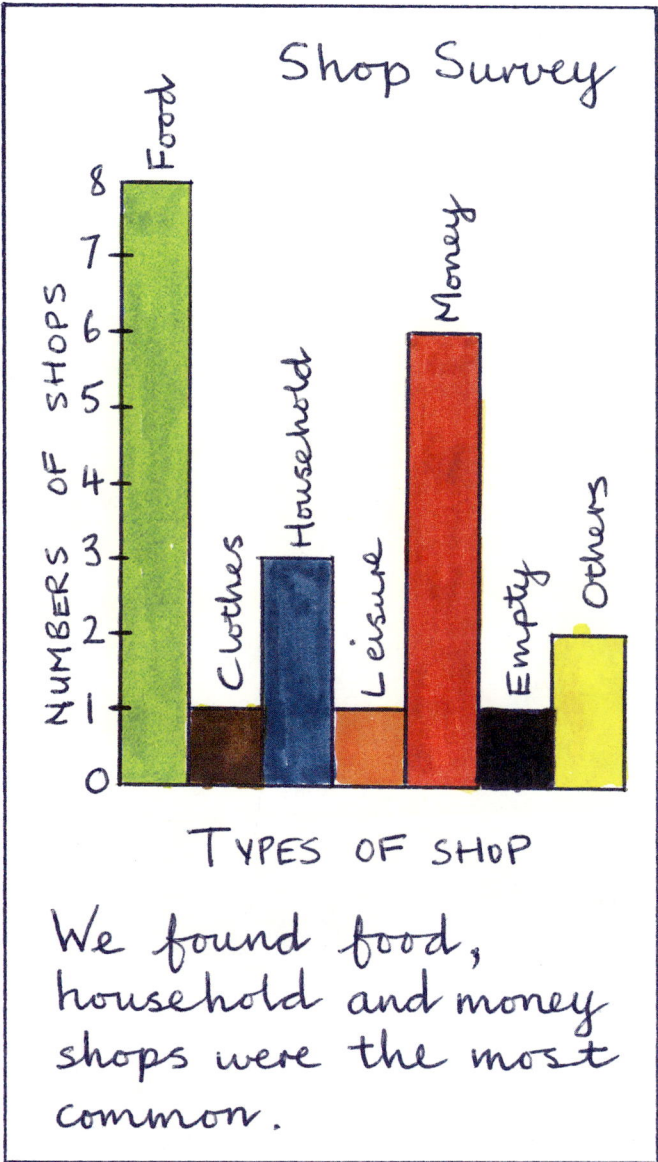

We found food, household and money shops were the most common.

Things to do ✂ - - - - - - - - - - - - -

Make a survey of the shops in a street near your school.

Shops in Benwell

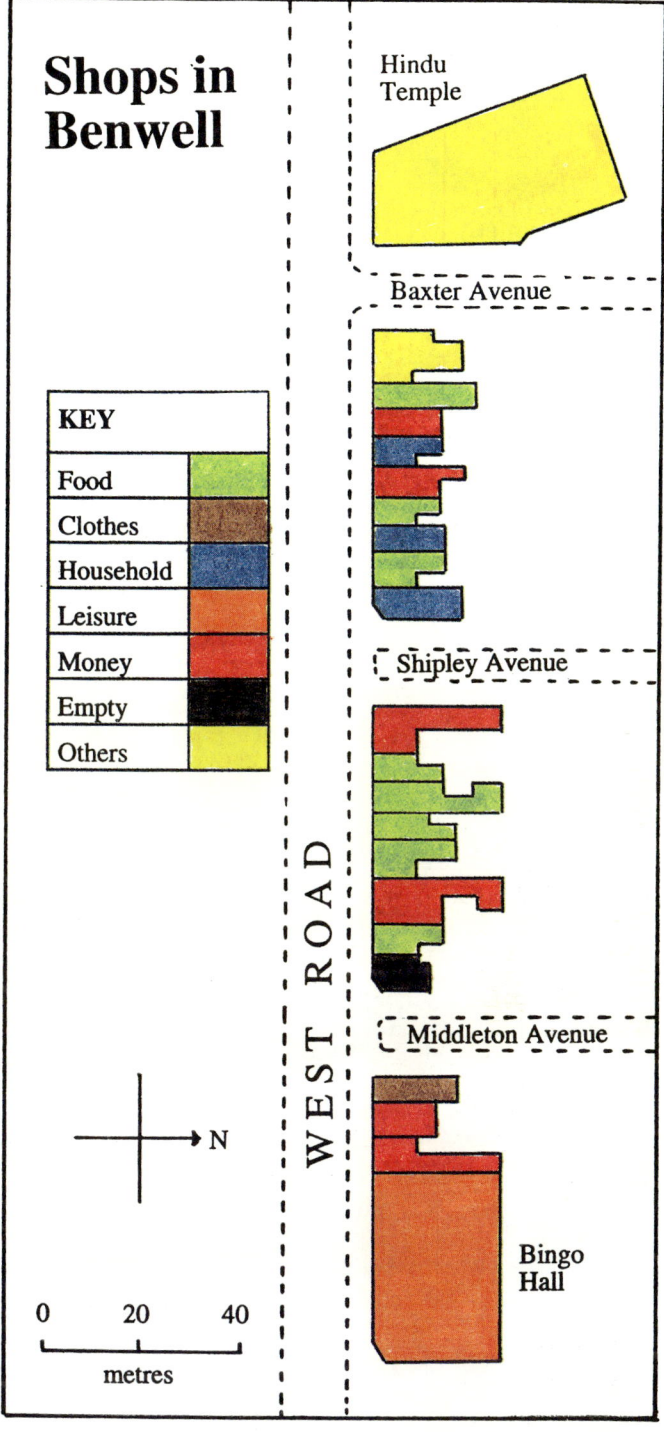

Environment

Pollution

What causes pollution?

When fumes, noise and waste cause damage to the environment it is called pollution. Some natural events cause pollution. For example, if a volcano explodes, it pollutes the air with large quantities of dust and poisonous gas. However, most forms of pollution are caused by people.

> ### *Talking and writing*
>
> 1 Make a class list of all the different types of pollution you can think of.
>
> 2 As a class, decide which type of pollution is the most serious?

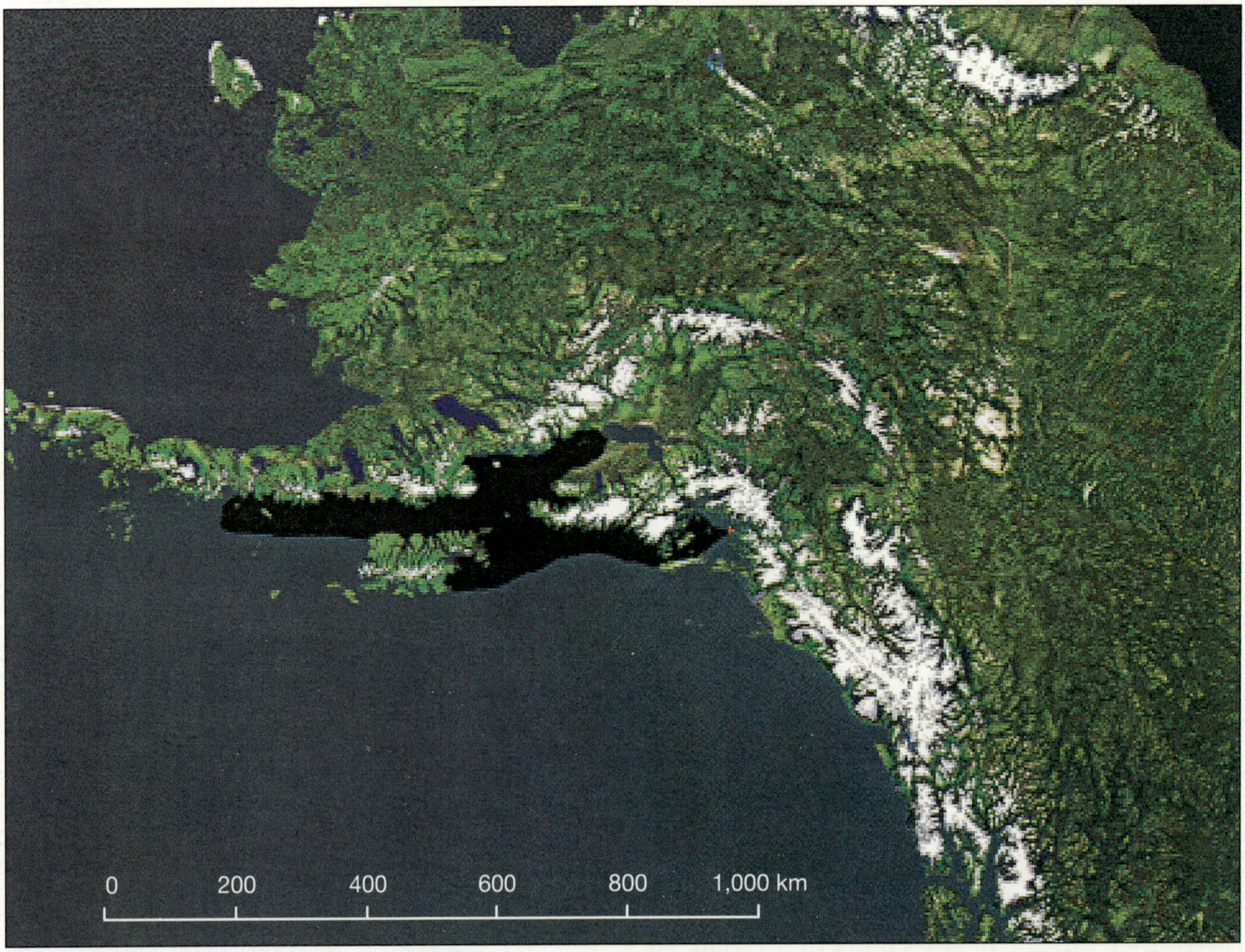

0   200   400   600   800   1,000 km

▲ *In March 1989, a huge oil tanker called the Exxon Valdez ran aground off the coast of Alaska in the USA. This satellite photograph shows how the oil spread down the coast after the accident.*

How do we cause pollution?

In the summer holidays we often go out for the day in the car.

We all like to go and visit places but cars clog up the roads and put poisonous fumes into the air.

I like getting presents at Christmas.

We all enjoy getting presents but some of the factories which make toys put chemicals into rivers.

I like eating crisps.

We all need to eat but the rubbish from food packets has to go somewhere.

Air pollution

Water pollution

Land pollution

How long does pollution last?

Pollution does not last forever. Fruit and vegetable peelings will rot in a few weeks. Paper and cardboard disappear in about a year. Metal lasts many years because it only rusts slowly. Plastic never rots.

▶ *This is the order in which things decay.*

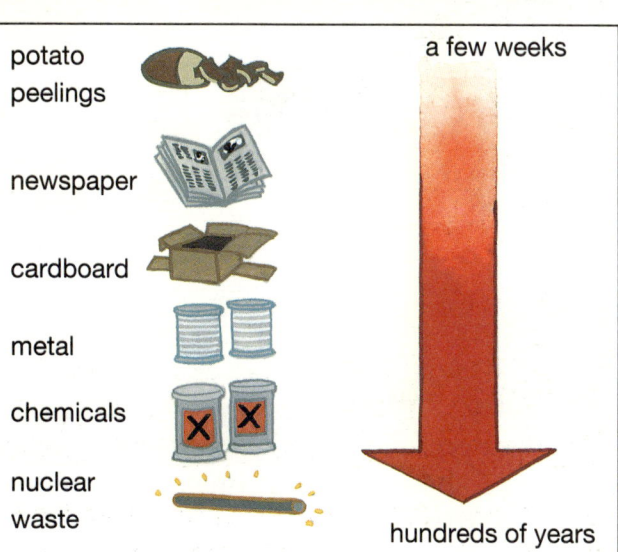

potato peelings

newspaper

cardboard

metal

chemicals

nuclear waste

a few weeks

hundreds of years

How can we reduce pollution?

We can all help to reduce pollution. We could buy fewer things which would save resources. We could also make sure that the things we no longer need are recycled.

Recently the government has passed new laws to protect the environment. The trouble is that it takes a long time for people to change their habits.

Recycling aluminium cans

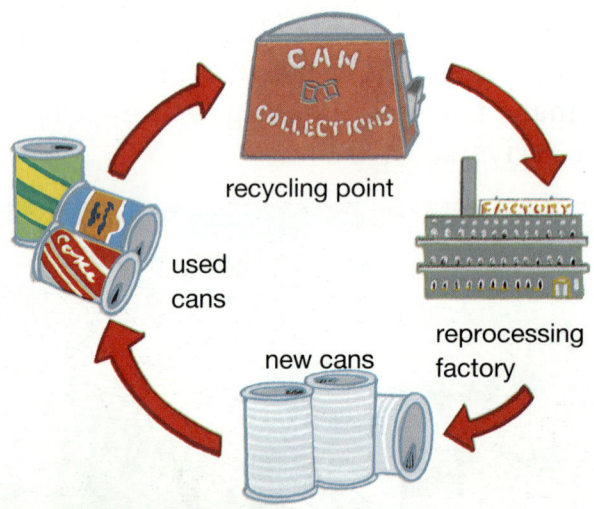

recycling point

used cans

reprocessing factory

new cans

The metal from old aluminium cans can be saved and used again. The same amount of energy makes 20 recycled cans or one new one.

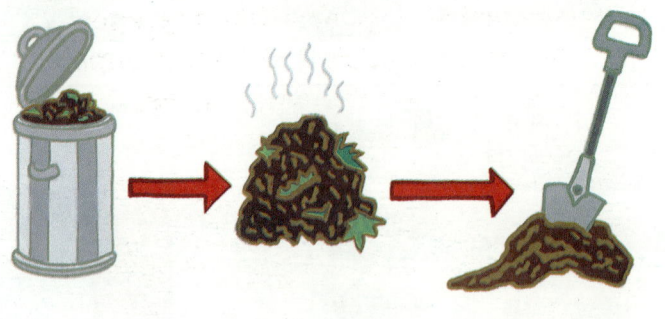

compost bin   compost heap   new soil

Making compost
Unwanted food rots down to make compost. This can be spread on the garden to keep the soil healthy.

Travelling by foot or by bike

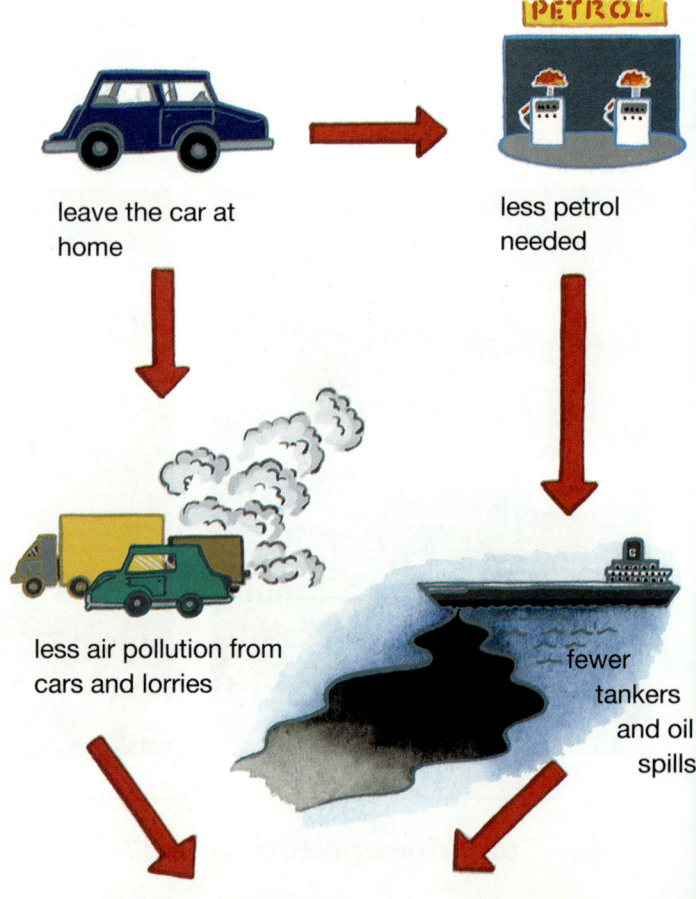

leave the car at home

less petrol needed

less air pollution from cars and lorries

fewer tankers and oil spills

Walking and cycling use only human energy. Cars and buses need fuel to run their engines and their exhust fumes pollute the air.

cleaner environment

Using the evidence

1 Design a poster which will encourage people to think of ways of reducing pollution.

2 Make a list of other ways of reducing pollution.

Using 'green' goods

Washing powder and weed killer sometimes contain harmful chemicals. We can buy alternatives which do less damage to the environment.

Saving energy
If everyone switches off lights they do not need and turns down the heating thermostat in their homes, it would save a lot of energy.

Renewable energy

There are ways of making electricity which cause very little pollution. These make use of natural forces, like the heat of the sun and the power of the wind. They are known as renewable sources because they will never run out, unlike coal, oil and gas.

Hydro-electric power
Hydro-electric power catches the energy from rivers as they flow downhill. Water is trapped by a dam to make a reservoir. The water is then used to turn a turbine to make electricity.

▲ *The Shasta Hydro-Electric Dam, USA.*

Wind farms
In some exposed places, like marshes and the tops of hills, there are groups of windmills. When the wind blows, it turns the blades and makes electricity.

▲ *A wind farm in California, USA.*

Drax power station

The power station.

Drax power station in North Yorkshire is the largest coal-fired power station in western Europe. It supplies electricity to homes and factories throughout England. Each day ten goods trains arrive at Drax to deliver the 38,000 tonnes of coal that are needed to keep the power station running.

The coal is burnt in boilers to make steam for the turbines. However, the coal also produces large amounts of smoke, ash and waste heat. At Drax they have found ways of solving these problems so that the power station no longer causes so much damage to the environment.

Problems	Solutions
Smoke from the chimneys goes into the air causing acid rain.	Limestone and water are sprayed on to the smoke to remove the fumes. The limestone turns into a mineral which is used to make plaster, cement and wall boards for houses.
The coal produces nearly two million tonnes of ash a year.	The ash is taken by conveyor to wasteland nearby. Bulldozers spread it out, soil is put on top and the land can then used for farming. Trees have been planted to make a nature reserve.
The turbines produce a lot of steam.	The steam is cooled and the warm air is used to heat nearby greenhouses. The greenhouses contain 350,000 tomato plants. The tomatoes they produce are sold in shops.

A local investigation

Pollution affects every part of the United Kingdom. Some children decided to investigate problems in their local area. They used the survey sheet opposite. First they identified the problems by circling the number in the correct column and then they added up the total. The score told the children how badly their local environment suffered from pollution. As they did the work the children also took photographs and made a map for a class display.

◀ *Noise from the lorry depot.*

◀ *Fumes from traffic waiting at the level crossing.*

◀ *Fumes from the petrol store.*

Pollution survey

Problem	No problem	Some	A lot
Traffic exhaust	0	5	(10)
Factory fumes	0	5	(10)
Traffic noise	0	5	(10)
Aircraft noise	(0)	5	10
Polluted water	0	(5)	10
Litter	0	(5)	10
Overhead wires	0	(5)	10
Unpleasant smells	0	5	(10)
Factory noise	0	(5)	10
Vandalism/graffiti	(0)	5	10
Total		60	

0	25	50 or more
No pollution	Some pollution	A lot of pollution

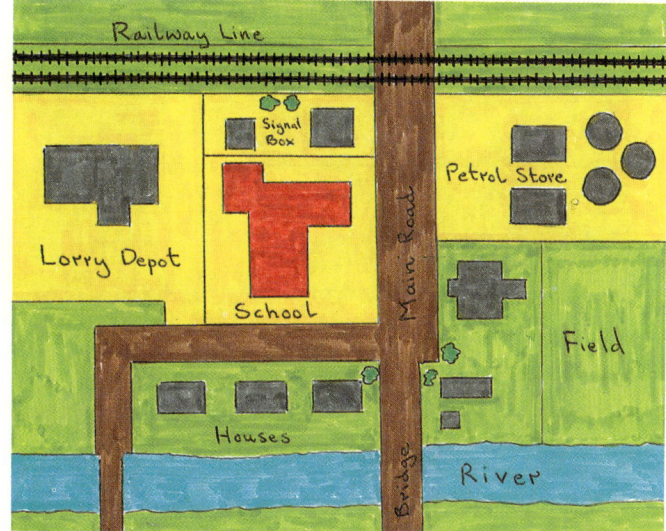

Things to do - - - - - - - - - - - - - -

Make a survey of pollution problems around your school.

United Kingdom

Wales

What is Wales like?

Wales is a country of hills, mountains, moors and valleys. It lies to the west of England and is about 200 kilometres long and 100 kilometres wide.

In the past there used to be a lot of mines in Wales. Roof slates for houses came from mines in the mountains of North Wales. Coal for factories, ships and train engines came from South Wales. Today the mines have closed and new industries have taken their place.

Two out of every three people in Wales live in the south of the country. In Central Wales, people live in small towns, scattered villages and farms. In the north, the main settlements are on the coast where tourism is important.

▲ Harlech Castle in North Wales. The castle was built by Edward I in 1285.

CROESO Y CYMRU

▲ This sign says 'Welcome to Wales'. In some parts of Wales, Welsh is the main language.

Scale
0 — 50 — 100 km

over 500 metres
200 - 500 metres
0 - 200 metres
sea

N

Holyhead
Anglesey
● Bangor
▲ Snowdon (1085 m)

Cader Idris (892 m) ▲

Irish Sea

CAMBRIAN MOUNTAINS

River Wye

River Severn

Fishguard
WALES

Milford Haven

Swansea
Port Talbot
Newport
Cardiff

Bristol Channel

Rivers and landscape
- Snowdon and Cader Idris in the Cambrian Mountains are the highest peaks in Wales.
- The Wye is the longest river (209 km).
- Anglesey is an island off the north-west coast.

Transport
- The main airport is at Cardiff.
- The M4 motorway links Wales and England via the Severn Bridge.
- Ferries sail to Ireland from the ports of Fishguard and Holyhead.

Weather
- Most parts of Wales have a high rainfall.
- Strong winds affect the coast and other exposed places.
- On the highest mountains, snow lasts all winter.

Settlement
- Cardiff is the capital city.
- Swansea and Newport are important ports on the Bristol Channel.
- Bangor is a seaside resort on the north coast.

Work
- Most of the factories are in South Wales. There are steelworks at Newport and Port Talbot and a large oil refinery at Milford Haven.
- In the mountains, most farmers keep sheep. There are dairy farms in the lowlands and valleys.
- Forestry is important in hilly areas in North and Central Wales.

▲ *The Port Talbot steelworks.*

▲ *Children pony-trekking in the Snowdonia National Park.*

Talking and writing

Talk about each of the places shown on the map of Wales. What can you learn about them from the information on this page? Write down your answers.

The story of Blaenavon

Blaenavon today

Blaenavon

Blaenavon is an industrial town about 40 kilometres north of Cardiff, high in the mountains of South Wales. The name Blaenavon means 'the source of the river' in Welsh.

In 1789, during the Industrial Revolution, three furnaces were built at Blaenavon to make use of local supplies of coal and ironstone. Within a few years the furnaces were producing thousands of tonnes of iron. By 1800, the first coal mines had opened with shafts going down into the ground.

People came from different parts of Wales and England to work at Blaenavon. The town grew larger as rows of stone cottages were built on the hillsides.

In 1852, in Victorian times, a railway was opened which linked Blaenavon with Newport docks. A large new colliery was also built. It was called Big Pit because it had a wide lift shaft. The coal from Big Pit was excellent quality. It burnt with a great heat and left very little ash. The coal was used as fuel for ships and railway engines all over the world.

▼ The ironworks in about 1800.

▼ Big Pit in the early 1900s when demand for coal was at its highest.

46

In the 1920s and 1930s everything changed. There was less demand for coal and many miners lost their jobs. The iron and steelworks closed which made more people unemployed. However, the coal mine was modernised and mining continued until 1980.

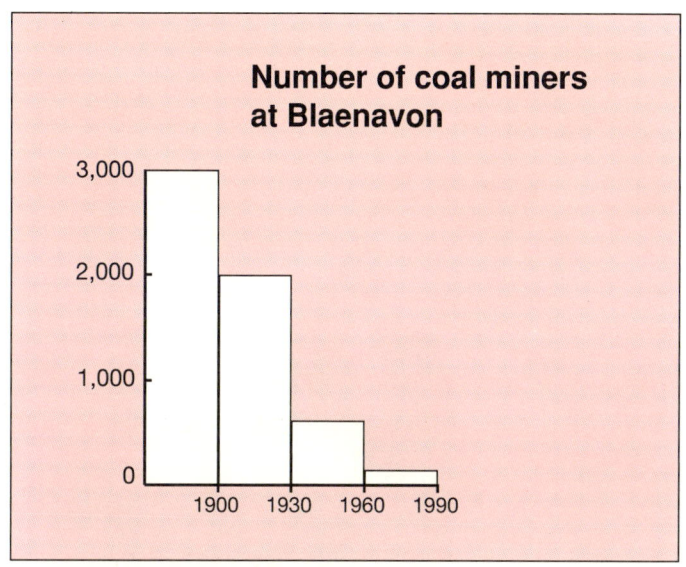

Number of coal miners at Blaenavon

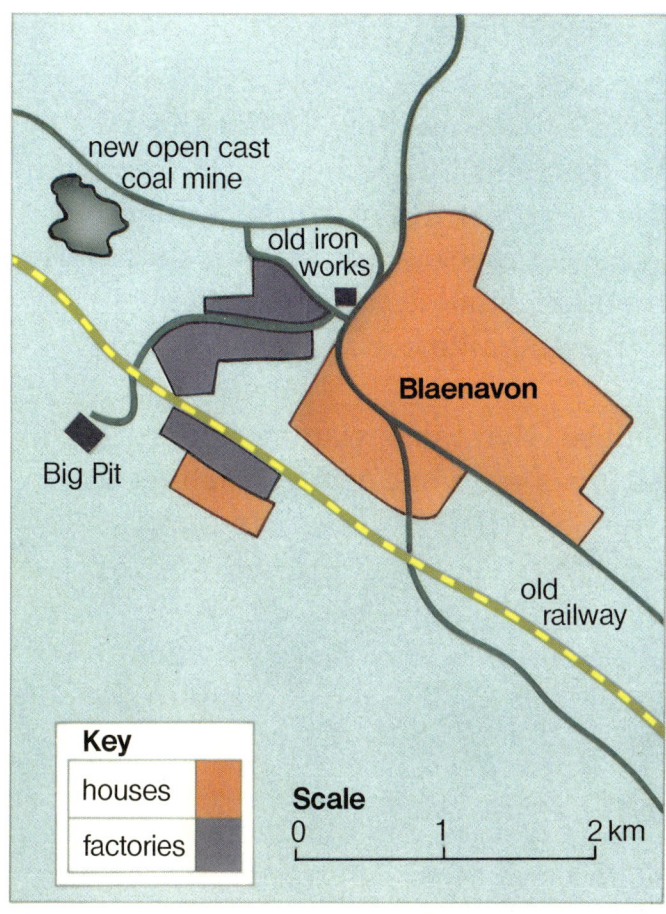

Today Blaenavon has a population of about 6,000 people. The most important factory makes parts for aeroplanes and employs 200 people. Other factories were built on the edge of the town in the 1960s. Since then a new trading estate has been opened. Some of the new companies received money from the government and the European Union to help them start up. In 1983, Big Pit was turned into a coal-mining museum. It now attracts thousands of visitors.

▲ One of the four chapels in Blaenavon.

▲ As people leave the town, shops are closing down.

▲ Most people live in terraced houses built in Victorian times.

A visit to Big Pit

Glyn Davies used to work at Big Pit. He left school when he was 15 to work in the mine. For many years, he repaired the steel ropes which were used to pull the lift up and down. Now he is a museum guide.

Before Glyn takes visitors underground, he gives everyone a safety helmet to wear. The helmet has a cap lamp. He also gives each visitor a self-rescuer just like the miners used to wear. Then everyone gets into the cage which quickly drops 90 metres down to the bottom of the shaft.

It is very dark and musty in the mine. "There are 40 kilometres of tunnels in Big Pit. They are held up with wooden props, bricks and steel arches," Glyn says.

"It was very important to get fresh air into the mine," Glyn explains. "A fan and ventilation doors helped to get rid of dangerous gases."

▲ *At the start of a visit to Big Pit.*

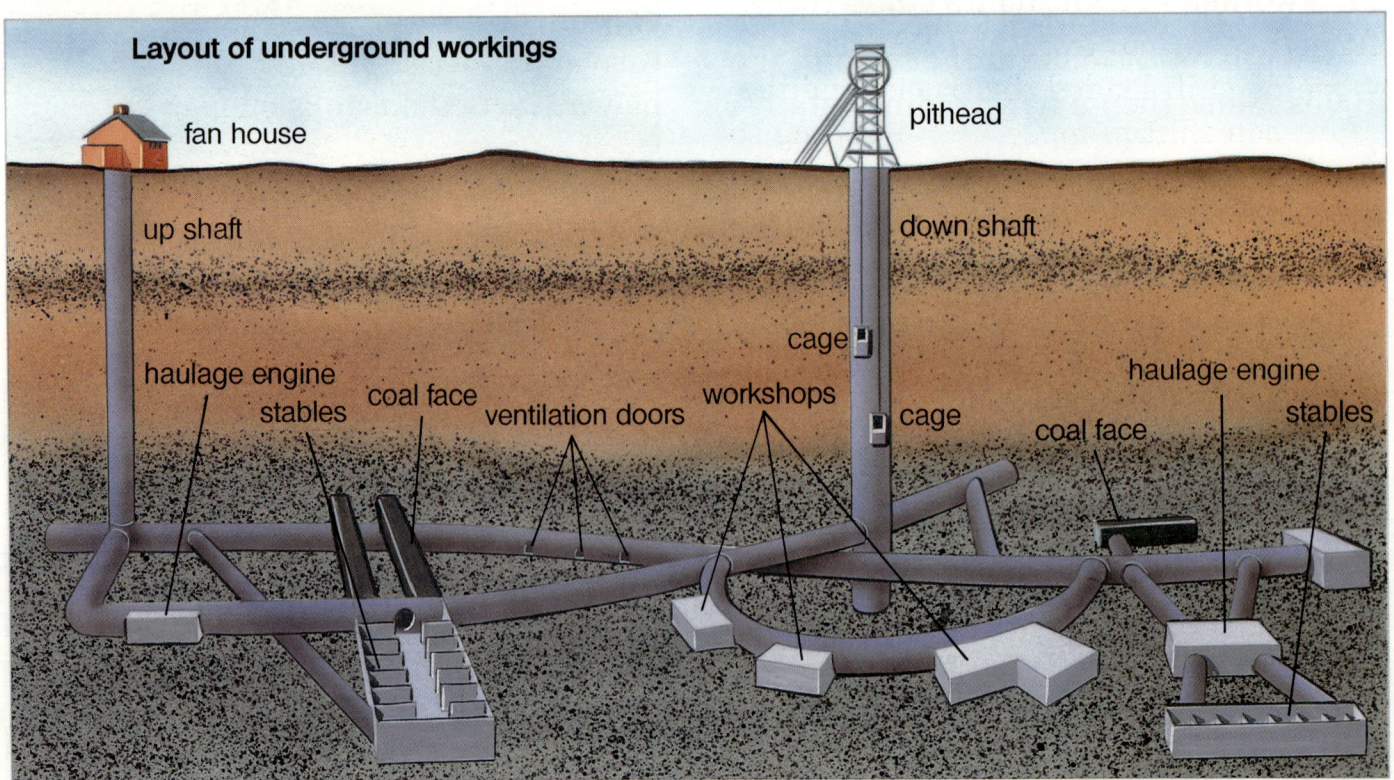

Layout of underground workings

fan house

pithead

up shaft

down shaft

cage

haulage engine

stables

coal face

ventilation doors

workshops

cage

haulage engine

coal face

stables

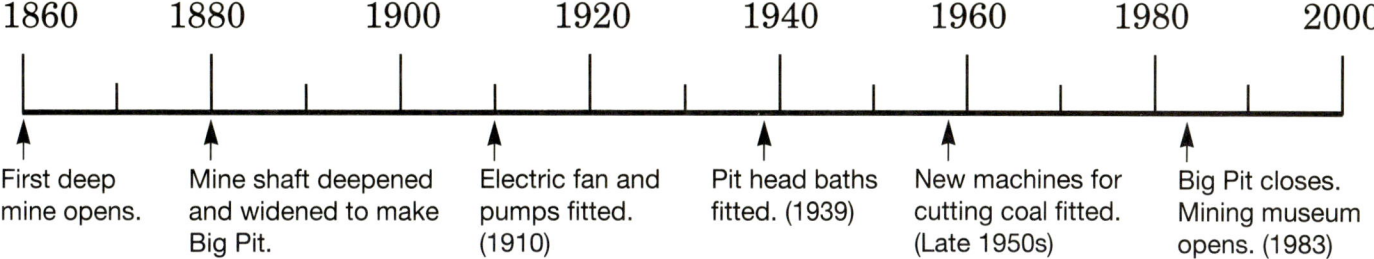

1860   1880   1900   1920   1940   1960   1980   2000

First deep mine opens.

Mine shaft deepened and widened to make Big Pit.

Electric fan and pumps fitted. (1910)

Pit head baths fitted. (1939)

New machines for cutting coal fitted. (Late 1950s)

Big Pit closes. Mining museum opens. (1983)

Glyn takes the visitors along the tunnels. He shows them the trucks that carried the coal and the rails they ran along. In some places, the ceiling is so low that everyone has to bend down. Water drips from the roof and streams run along gutters on the ground. The rocks are stained orange from the iron in the water. At one point, Glyn asks everyone to turn out their lamps. It is very dark. Then Glyn takes the visitors to the stables. In the past there were over 70 ponies at Big Pit. They lived in the dark all their lives and were used to pull the coal trucks.

Finally the visitors come to the coal face. Men worked in eight hours shifts there. At night they cut away the coal. The morning shift loaded the trucks and the afternoon shift propped up the ceiling so the new tunnel would be safe. It was a dangerous job and dust used to get into the miners' lungs which made them ill.

"As far as I am concerned," Glyn says, "the coal from Big Pit was the finest in the world. Also we had very few accidents. The problem was that the coal seams ran out so the mine had to close. It was tough work but I am proud to have been a miner."

▲ Glyn takes a group of visitors along one of the tunnels.

Things to do ✂ - - - - - - - - - - - - -

1 Make a timeline showing six changes in the history of Blaenavon. Start with ironmaking in 1789.

2 What is being done to help people in Blaenavon now that Big Pit is no longer a coal mine?

3 How has the place where you live changed in the last 200 years?

You have learnt

◆ what makes Wales different from other countries in the United Kingdom
◆ about the workings of a coal mine
◆ how some parts of Wales are changing.

Greece

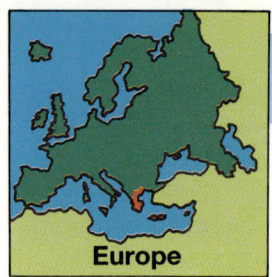

Europe

What is Greece like?

Long ago, one of the oldest civilizations began in the country we now call Greece. Three thousand years ago, the ancient Greeks built beautiful temples, statues and theatres. They also made important discoveries in science, mathematics and other subjects. People have admired and copied their ideas ever since. The Olympic Games were first held by the ancient Greeks and now take place every four years.

Today Greece is one of the countries of the European Union. The Greek mainland links up with Albania, Bulgaria and other countries to the north. There are also hundreds of Greek islands scattered across the Aegean Sea. The islands are popular with tourists in the summer. People come from all over northern Europe to enjoy the sunshine.

BULGARIA

MACEDONIA

TURKEY

ALBANIA

PINDUS MOUNTAINS

●Thessaloniki

GREECE

TURKEY

Aegean Sea

N

Patras●

Piraeus●■Athens

Ionian Sea

Corinth Canal

Amorgos

Scale

| 0 | 100 | 200 | 300 km |

Crete

over 1,000 metres
200 - 1,000 metres
0 - 200 metres
Sea

Landscape

Much of Greece is covered by rocky mountains. These reach out into the sea as headlands and chains of islands.

▲ *The Pindus Mountains.*

Settlement

One in three people live in Athens, the capital city. Piraeus and Thessaloniki are the main ports.

Transport

Road and rail routes tend to follow the coast. Ferries link the islands with the mainland.

▲ *The Corinth Canal was opened in 1893. Large ships use it to sail between the Aegean and Ionian Seas.*

Weather

Greece has a Mediterranean climate which means that there is plenty of rain in winter but the summers are hot and dry.

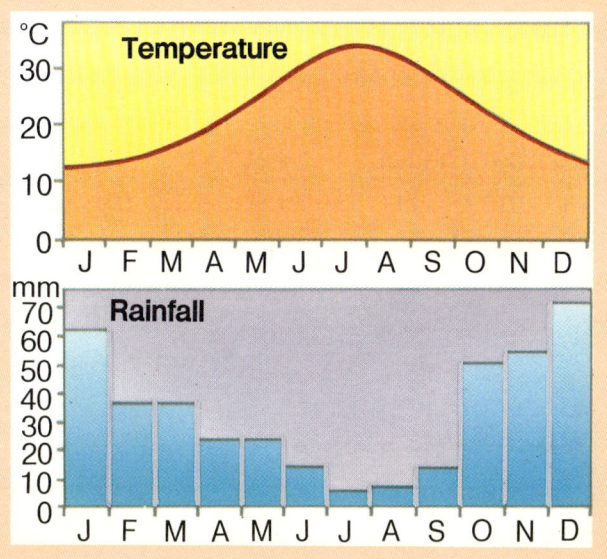

Work

In the towns, factories make metals, chemicals, clothes and electronic goods. Wheat, tobacco, tomatoes and fruit are the main farm crops. Tourism is also important.

▲ *Everyone in the family helps to harvest the olives.*

Talking and writing

In what ways is Greece different from the United Kingdom?

Summer in Athens

Dimitra lives in Athens in a large flat with her mother, father, grandmother, brother and sister. Her school is five minutes walk away. Lessons start at 8.00 am and end at 1.00 pm. Everyone takes a long break from work in the afternoon because it gets very hot at this time of day. Between 4.00 pm and 6.00 pm when it is cooler, Dimitra has extra lessons and does her homework. She goes to bed at 10.00 pm.

▲ *Dimitra with her family on Amorgos.*

Dimitra's day

sleep	school	lunch and sleep	extra lessons	play or watch TV	sleep
midnight 8.00 am	1.00 pm	4.00 pm	6.00 pm	10.00 pm	

▼ *In Athens, modern blocks of flats now surround the hill where the ancient Greeks built their temple.*

Each year, at the end of June, Dimitra goes to stay with her cousins on the island of Amorgos. This is a good time to leave Athens because the fumes from the traffic and the heat of the sun cause a terrible smog. The Greeks call it *nefos*. Sometimes the *nefos* is so bad people are forbidden to use their cars.

Dimitra and her family travel by taxi to Piraeus to catch the ferry. At first, their journey takes them through the modern part of Athens where there are lots of office blocks and hotels. Then they go past the museum and the parliament building in Syntagma Square.

Ahead of them, on top of a rocky hill, are the ruins of a famous temple called the Parthenon. This was part of a fortress which was built by the ancient Greeks about 2,500 years ago. Looking through the taxi window, Dimitra can see the old houses and narrow streets of the old town, or plaka. There are open-air markets and ancient buildings. When they went to Amorgos last year a wind called the *meltemi* was blowing in the Aegean and the sea was very rough. "I hope it won't be too windy for you today," the taxi driver says.

◀ *Taxis in Syntagma Square, Athens.*

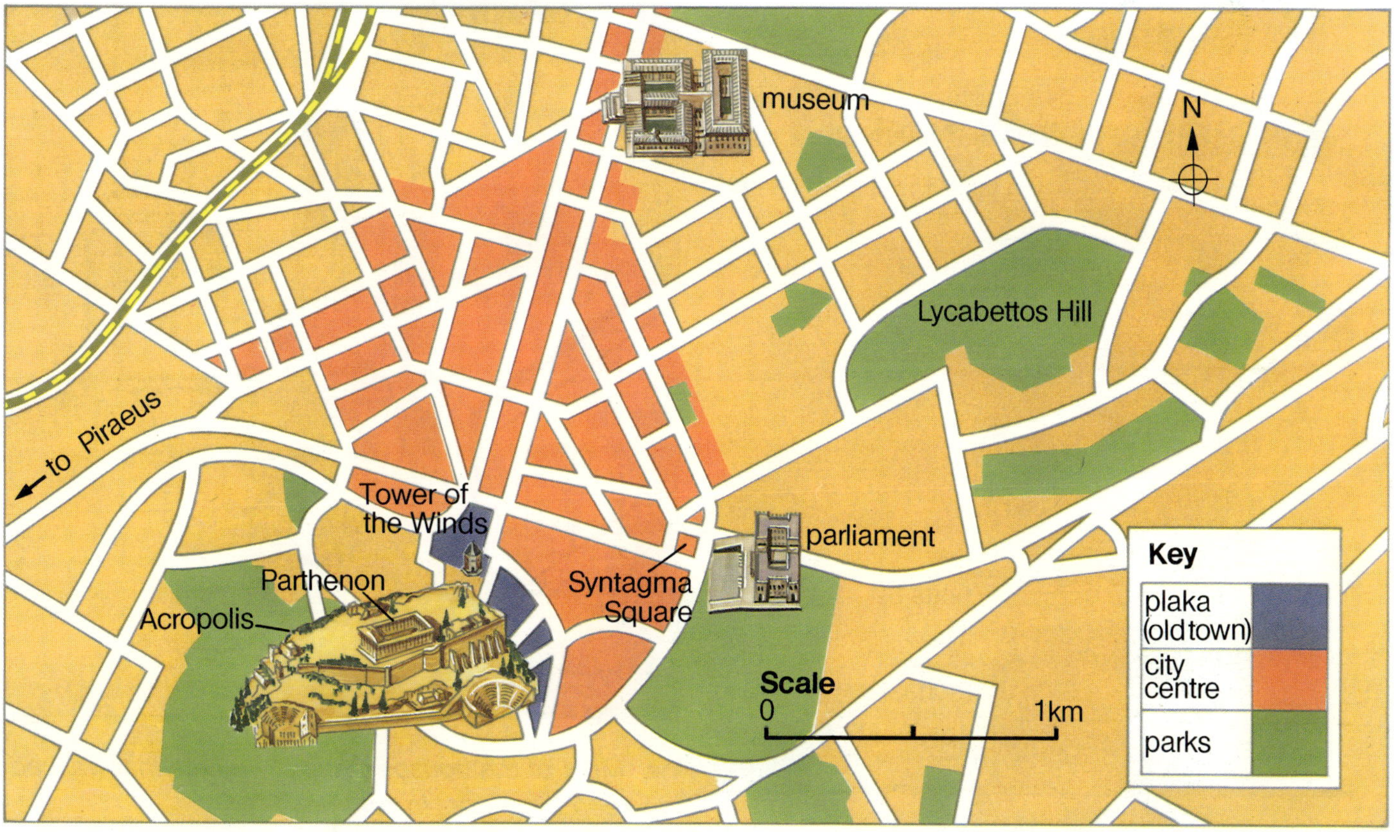

Visiting Amorgos

At last the taxi reaches Piraeus. Dimitra had forgotten how busy it is. There are a lot of ferries, all being loaded with cars and lorries. "You can go to over 60 islands from here," her father tells her. "Our ferry will take about 11 hours to reach Amorgos. It's a long way and we stop at four other islands before we get there."

Amorgos is about 35 kilometres long and 6 kilometres wide. The countryside is rocky with steep hillsides. Drivers have to be careful on the narrow road that runs from the north to the south of the island.

▲ *Most of the ferries which go to the islands leave from Piraeus harbour.*

Dimitra's cousins live in a fishing port called Egiali. It has a large harbour and a wide sandy beach. The town is built on a hill and has narrow streets and alleyways with steep steps.

▲ *Most of the houses in the town are whitewashed to keep them cool in summer.*

54

▲ Lunch at the taverna.

▲ Dimitra's collection of things which remind her of the holidays.

Dimitra's uncle owns a taverna near the beach. In the summer, the taverna is busy with tourists who want a cool drink or a meal. Running the taverna keeps the whole family busy. Dimitra's aunt does the cooking. Her cousin, Marios, takes the orders. Sometimes Dimitra helps to make up salads of tomatoes, cucumbers, olives and cheese. Her uncle goes out fishing so fresh fish is always on the menu. Occasionally he takes some tourists out with him in the boat and leaves them for a few hours on one of the beaches for a picnic.

Dimitra always finds something new to do. Last year she went to a cousin's wedding at the village of Tholaria. People danced through the streets as part of the celebrations and they roasted a lamb on a spit.

Things to do - - - - - - - - - - - - -

1 Copy the timeline showing how Dimitra spends her day in Athens. Leave a space underneath for a second timeline and write in the things you normally do.

2 Use the map to follow Dimitra's route through Athens. Make drawings of the landmarks she passes. Put them in the correct order.

3 Write down three things you think Dimitra could tell you about a) living in Athens, and b) visiting Amorgos.

You have learnt

◆ about the environment of Greece
◆ what it is like to live in Athens
◆ about the Greek islands

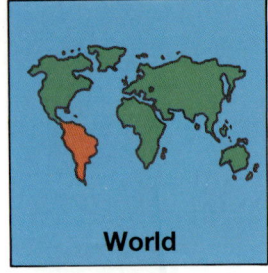

South America

What is South America like?

South America is joined to North and Central America and stretches southwards towards Antarctica. The Andes mountains run down the western edge of the continent. In the Andes there are many snowy peaks and volcanoes. Some of the volcanoes are still active. The Amazon is the main river. It rises in the Andes and flows for 6,440 kilometres before it enters the Atlantic Ocean at the Equator.

South America is divided into 13 countries. Brazil is much bigger than any of the others and covers half the continent. The main cities are along the coast of Brazil and Argentina. There are large parts of South America where very few people live.

During the sixteenth century the Spanish and Portuguese came to South America looking for gold and silver. The Portuguese settled in the north east which is why Portuguese is spoken in Brazil today. The Spanish settled in the other parts of the continent so Spanish is the main language everywhere else.

▲ *The modern part of Buenos Aires, Argentina, has wide, tree-lined avenues.*

▲ *Bolivian women on a mountain trail.*

Map labels

Panama Canal

River Orinoco

Angel Falls

Equator

River Amazon

PERU

SOUTH AMERICA

BRAZIL

Lima

ANDES MOUNTAINS

Lake Titicaca

BOLIVIA

N

Pacific Ocean

River Paraguay

Rio de Janeiro

São Paulo

Mt Aconcagua

Buenos Aires

ARGENTINA

Atlantic Ocean

Key

mountains	
deserts	
grasslands	
mixed forests	
rainforest	

Scale

0   1,000   2,000   3,000   4,000 km

Talking and writing

Draw your own map of South America. Name five features or places and write a sentence about each one.

Fact file

◆ The River Amazon carries four times as much water as any other river.

◆ Mount Aconcagua in Argentina is the highest peak in the Andes (6,960 metres).

◆ Lake Titicaca, between Peru and Bolivia, is the largest lake in South America. It is also the highest lake in the world on which ships sail (3,811 metres).

◆ The Angel Falls in Venezuela are the highest waterfalls in the world (979 metres).

◄ A tributary of the River Amazon winding through the rainforest.

57

The Amazon rainforest

The Amazon rainforest is nearly as large as Europe. Vast numbers of different plants and animals thrive in the hot, wet climate. Many of the plants that grow in the rainforest are very useful to us. Rice, cacao, peanuts, oranges, lemons, tea and coffee all come from the rainforest.

Groups of American Indians and rubber tappers used to be the only people who lived in the rainforest. Today things are changing. The forest is disappearing fast. Each year, large areas are cleared to make space for new cattle ranches. Loggers with their heavy vehicles drive tracks deep into the forest looking for teak and other trees they can sell for high prices. Elsewhere, mines and factories have opened and new roads have been built.

"Today everyone wants to make money out of the Amazon, and we are scared. Scared by the burning that is taking place, by the destruction that is taking place, by the pollution.
I speak as a person who has lived all his life in the forest."
Leader of the Kayapo Indians.

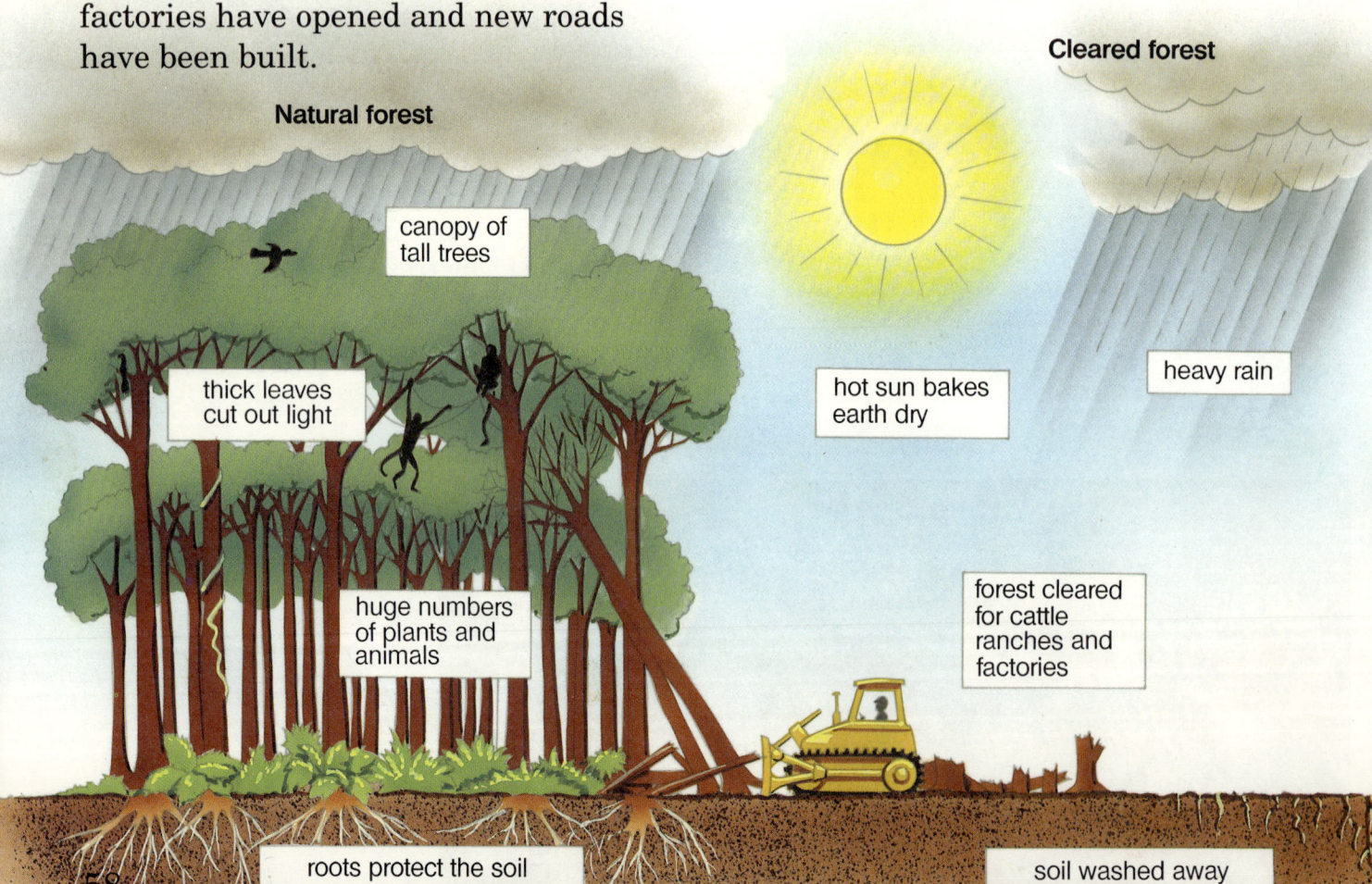

Natural forest

Cleared forest

canopy of tall trees

hot sun bakes earth dry

heavy rain

thick leaves cut out light

huge numbers of plants and animals

forest cleared for cattle ranches and factories

roots protect the soil

soil washed away

Living in the rainforest

My name is José. I live in the rainforest in Brazil. My father is a rubber tapper. He goes out into the forest early each morning to collect sap from the rubber trees. Sometimes I go with him.

There are over 100,000 families like us in Brazil. The forest provides us with food, the materials to build houses and most of the other things we need. We use the trees without damaging them.

We live in a wooden house.

We grow rice, maize and manioc (which is like potatoes) in a forest clearing.

In the evening, my father lights a fire. The smoke turns the latex into rubber.

When my father comes to a rubber tree, he cuts the bark and collects the sap, called latex, in a cup.

We see snakes, monkeys and other animals in the forest.

Sometimes my father shoots a bird or an animal for dinner.

My mother knows all the plants we can use as medicines.

Palm trees provide the thatch for the house roof.

We collect coconuts, avocados or other fruit from trees along the trail.

Using the evidence

1 How is José's family able to survive in the forest?

2 What could change José's way of life?

Chico Mendes

Chico Mendes was a rubber tapper. In 1988 he was murdered on the steps of his home in Brazil because he tried to save the rainforests. Thousands of people from all over the world went to his funeral. This is his life story.

1944

❶ My life began like that of all rubber tappers. I never went to school and started work when I was nine years old.

1962

❷ When I was 18 I was taught to read and write by a rubber tapper who lived alone in the forest. We used to listen to the radio to find out what was happening in the world. Every night we talked about what we had heard.

❸ I realised we needed to save the rainforest. The landowners were busy cutting and burning down the trees and building ranches for cattle. This was destroying the forest. In 1974 I joined the Rubber Workers Union. We met the leaders of the local American Indian groups and they agreed to help as well.

1968

1974

1985

❹ We asked the government to set up reserves. We wanted people to find ways of using the forest without damaging it.

1987

❺ In 1987, the plantation where I worked was sold to a man called Da Silva. He tried to drive us off the land so he could build a ranch. We stood firm and the government made it into a reserve.

1988

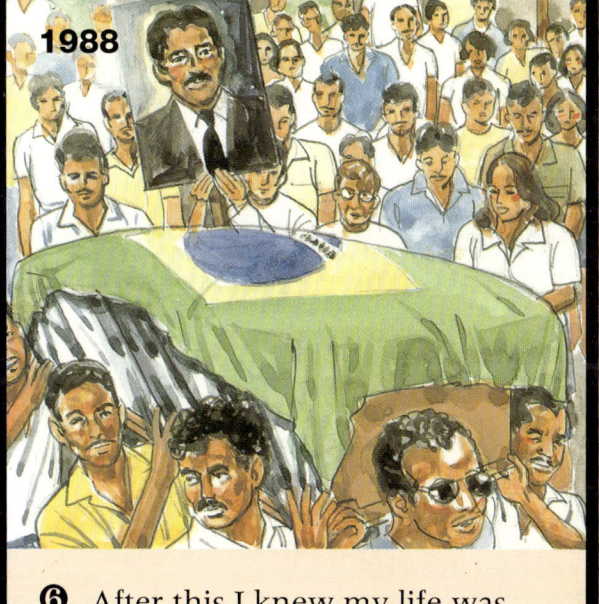

❻ After this I knew my life was in danger. Da Silva hired a gang of gunmen. However, even if I am killed the protest will go on.

Things to do - - - - - - - - - - - - - -

1 Make a timeline showing the different things which happened to Chico Mendes.

2 Write a letter telling the government why they need to make more reserves.

You have learnt

◆ about the landscape and people of South America
◆ what is happening to the rainforest
◆ how the rainforest could be protected.

Glossary

acid rain	Polluted rain which damages the environment and affects people's health.
climate	The pattern of weather over many years.
continent	Great blocks of land, such as Africa.
crop	Plants that farmers harvest, like bananas.
delta	Flat land at the mouth of a river.
environment	The world around us.
Equator	An imaginary line around the Earth, half-way between the North and South Poles.
factory	A place where goods are made so they can be sold.
fumes	Harmful gases which damage the health of people, plants and animals.
importer	Someone who brings goods into a country to sell.
mineral	Materials like gold and silver which are found naturally in earth and rocks.
monsoon	A season of heavy rain which comes after dry weather in South-East Asia and other parts of the world.
moorland	Hills that are covered with heather or grass and have very few trees.
ocean	A huge expanse of deep water between the continents.
planet	A mass of rock and gas which circles around a star or a sun.
plantation	A large farm where only one crop is grown.
pollution	Changes in our surroundings which damage the health of people, plants or animals.
rainforest	Areas of thick forest which are near to the Equator.
recycle	To use something again.
reservoir	A lake where water is stored.
resource	Something which people find useful.
river channel	The route a river takes.
season	Times of the year when there is a particular type of weather.
settlement	The places where people live, such as houses, towns and cities.
sewage	The waste which is carried away from buildings in pipes.
tourism	Arranging holidays and visits for people.
traders	People who buy and sell goods.
trading estate	A place where offices and warehouses are grouped together.
transport	The vehicles used by people or goods.
tributary	A stream or river that flows into a larger river.
weather	The wetness, wind, heat and cold in the air around us.

Index

Published by Collins Educational,
An imprint of HarperCollins*Publishers*
77-85 Fulham Palace Road, London W6 8JB

First published 1995

987654321

ISBN 0 00 315 472 6

Printed and bound in Italy by Printer Trento s.r.l.

Designed by Chi Leung

Illustrations by Julian Baker Illustrations 4-5, 7, 10, 11, 12, 14, 16, 17, 18, 19, 22, 23, 25, 26-27, 28, 29, 30, 31, 34-35, 42, 44, 46, 47, 48, 50, 51, 53, 54, 56, 57, 58; Maggie Brand/Maggie Mundy p2; Joan Corlass pp59, 60-61; Jenny Mumford pp21, 39t; Karen Tushingham/Maggie Mundy pp2, 8, 14, 20 26, 32, 38, 39, 40-41

Picture research by Faith Perkins

Photographs reproduced by permission of:
(t=top b=bottom l=left r=right c=centre)

J Allan Cash pp32t, 51bl; Allsport p8 (Agence Vadystadt/Philippe Blondel); Big Pit pp46br, 48, 49; Celtic Picture Library pp44, 45l; COMSTOCK p11; James Davis Travel Photography p54b; Environmental Picture Library pp5b (Mike Jackson), 39l&c (Martin Bond), 39r (Robert Brook); FESA UK Ltd p34l&r; Field Studies Council (Tony Thomas) p13l&r; Frank Lane Picture Agency p9c (S McCutcheon); Terry Harris Photographs pp51tl, 51br, 52t, 53 and 55l; Hutchison Photograph Library p20 (Philip Wolmuth); IMAGE BANK UK p54t (David Hamilton); Terry Jewson pp35, 43; The Living Earth, Inc/Earth Imaging p38; NHPA p15 (EA Janes); National Power p42; Christine Osborne Pictures p23bl; PANOS Pictures p17 (Mike Krofchak); Planet Earth Pictures pp3t (Georgette Douwma), 3b (Robert Hessler), 5c (Doug Perrine), 6t (Linda Pitkin); Popperfoto p10t; QA Photos p27; Scarborough Borough Council p19t&l; Science Photo Library pp6c, 41t&b; South American Pictures pp56r (Tony Morrison), 56l (Frank Nowikowski), 57 & 60 (Tony Morrison); Stephen Scoffham pp33t, 46t, 47; Still Pictures pp3c & 4t (Mark Edwards); Telegraph Colour Library pp5t (Halary), 45r (S Benbow), 52b (VCL); Topham Picture Source p24t; TRIP p23c&br; Barry Waddams pp24ct, cb&b, 32b, 33b&background, 55r; Dr A Waltham p9t&b; A Wastell p19r; Welsh Industrial and Maritime Museum, Cardiff p46bl; Derek Widdicombe p18 (Pat Ruddle); ZEFA p16

Adapted extract on p17 from *Plain Tales from the Raj* by Charles Allen, published by Futura Paperbacks © 1975 by Charles Allen and the BBC

The authors and publishes would like to acknowledge with thanks the help given by the following people and organisations in the preparation of this book:
Big Pit; FESA; Antonia Lineham; Clive Stein; Tony Thomas, Field Studies Council; Marion Walter; Chris and Karen Young

Cover photograph: Eurostar train coming out of the Channel Tunnel
Reproduced courtesy of QA Photos